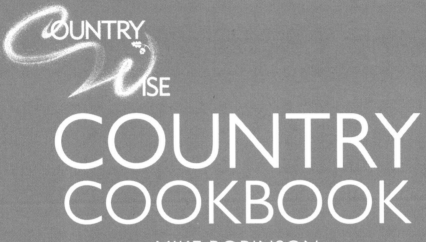

COUNTRY COOKBOOK

MIKE ROBINSON

itv

COUNTRY
COOKBOOK

MIKE ROBINSON

PAVILION

Countrywise Country Cookbook
As seen on ITV
www.itv.com

First published in the United Kingdom in 2011 by
PAVILION BOOKS
10 Southcombe Street, London W14 0RA
An imprint of Anova Books Company Ltd

Commissioning editor: Becca Spry
Art direction: Georgina Hewitt
Layout: Pene Parker
Photography: Kristin Perers
Food styling: Sam Head
Food styling Assistant: Kostas Stavrinos
Prop styling: Pene Parker
Editor: Barbara Dixon
Indexer: Hilary Bird
Production: Laura Brodie
ISBN: 9781862059320

A CIP catalogue record for this book is available from the British Library.

10 9 8 7 6 5 4 3 2 1

Colour reproduction by Mission, Hong Kong
Printed and bound by L.E.G.O. S.p.A. Italy
www.anovabooks.com

CONTENTS

INTRODUCTION

I consider myself to be the luckiest of men. I travel the country, foraging and cooking, for *Countrywise* and *Countrywise Kitchen*, and I live in an area that, in my opinion, is akin to paradise: west Berkshire. At home I use the fat of the land in a practical way, working as a modern-day hunter-gatherer and feeding customers at my pub, The Pot Kiln, so that everyone benefits. It is a privilege to present *Countrywise* and *Countrywise Kitchen* with Paul Heiney, for we get to eat the best the UK has to offer and to meet people who really know our country and what makes it tick.

It is amazing how much food is out there in this bounteous land of ours, and how well the land works when left to the devices of people who understand it. These people – the farmers, gamekeepers and fishermen – are the reason why *Countrywise* and *Countrywise Kitchen* exist; they are the cement that holds the British countryside together, and *Countrywise* is their programme.

'We have an amazingly diverse variety of landscapes and cultures on this postage stamp of an island. As a result, our foodstuffs change hugely across the length and breadth of the country.'

We have an amazingly diverse variety of landscapes and cultures on this postage stamp of an island. As a result, our foodstuffs change hugely across the length and breadth of the country. You cannot farm lamb in the same way on the rich downland of Hampshire as you would on the windswept and harsh uplands of the Outer Hebrides, for example, and yet we call the meat 'lamb' notwithstanding. We need to get the hang of provenance – that is, to know exactly what our food is and where it comes from.

There is a real change happening to the food culture in Britain. We, the Great British public, are demanding ever-higher standards from our food, and producers are responding as never before. I get very excited by the buzz at food markets and farm shops on a Saturday morning. And it is not only the small shops and markets – supermarkets are doing it, too.

This demand for ever-increasing quality has had a direct effect on farming practices. A few years ago we would have thought an organic chicken was really 'out there', but now we will pick up organic produce without giving it a second thought.

I believe that the biggest single change is our awareness of food ethics. Ethical food to me is food that achieves two goals. Firstly, for meat and fish, it should mean that the animal has had a good life and, crucially, a respectful end. Secondly, the land should suffer as little as possible from the raising of the food; I see daily how species such as the brown hare, one of our most beautiful and iconic mammals, have benefited from good modern farming techniques. No longer subject to toxic sprays, and allowed conservation strips that are left wild around fields, these creatures are doing really well. Wildlife in general owes much to the British farmer.

'We picked masses of heady scented wild garlic, wild hop shoots from the hedgerows and sundry other edibles that teemed wherever we looked.'

Another big change that has come about in recent years, and one that still has a long way to go, is our awareness of seasonality. Until 40 or so years ago we never gave it a second thought; we just ate food that was in season. You had asparagus in May, and that was that. The idea of buying it in December would never have entered people's minds. Modern transport techniques changed all that and now you can buy a product like asparagus all year round, albeit from Peru.

We are learning to embrace the seasonality of our foods and to make the most of the often short windows of opportunity. As I write this, the trees outside are bursting with elderflowers – one of the most wonderful tastes there is, but available only in a three-week window, which we made full use of in the past. Elderflower cordial is unbelievably easy to make and is basically the bottled and preserved sunshine of early summer. I make tons of it, just as I pick the sloes of Autumn and preserve them in gin for the cold Winter months.

Nowhere is this idea of seasonality so important as in the hunt for wild food. Foraging has become a buzzword as people enjoy the thrill of finding wild food, which is available in abundance in the UK.

I particularly enjoy foraging on the seashore. One of the beauties of our coastline, especially the cleaner parts such as north Devon, is that we can, with a little knowledge and the right feel for the environment, go and forage safely for the bounty to be found there. In this day and age of rules and regulations, there is a delight to be gained from finding a meal for free: it gives a childish pleasure and is an enjoyable form of hunting that people should try. All you need is a reference work (I like Roger Phillips' great book *Wild Food*, a photographic guide to every wild edible food in the UK, with its seasonality and general advice).

If you are going to join the millions who are thinking hard about how they eat, then you need to know your vegetables. Our temperate islands, protected from the savage Arctic cold by the Gulf Stream, grow some of the finest veg in the world, and thousands of artisan producers are growing amazing food in the soil. As a committed carnivore, I learned to love vegetables only when I took over the pub The Pot Kiln six years ago. Behind the pub we had a small piece of waste land that needed using, so we built some beds and engaged a local expert to help. Now our garden has a polytunnel, we use every inch of land we have and grow all our salads, most of our veg and a lot of herbs. To be able to walk out of the kitchen door and pick salad leaves 10 minutes before service is a real joy, and makes me feel like I am doing something worthwhile. The taste of food like this is unparalleled, since none of its flavour has been lost. You can get close to this by buying your veg when it comes into season, and not using imported produce. You can also, of course, start growing some of your own. You don't need a garden – window boxes are awesome for growing salads and carrots.

'Our temperate islands, protected from the savage Arctic cold by the Gulf Stream, grow some of the finest veg in the world, and thousands of artisan producers are growing amazing food in the soil.'

Seasonality is not just for the land, however. Fish, in both our seas and rivers, are seasonal. When filming fishing for *Countrywise* I am always struck by the love that fishermen have for what they do. On a memorable morning on a crab boat out of Lulworth Cove in Dorset, we caught a huge lobster, and I mean *huge* – this old fellow must have been 100 years old and weighed about seven kilos. The fisherman looked at it with real affection and mentioned that he caught it about four times a year. There was not even a thought of killing such a fabulous creature, and back into the sea it went. These people are the real conservationists – they appreciate that if they take too much, their livelihood will be gone. A good example of this is the wonderful Randolph Jenkins, with whom I filmed on the Gower Peninsula in south Wales. What a place! Miles of sandy beach, which Randolph has walked for 60 years. His particular skill is in finding the area's buried treasure: the cockle. I love these humble little shellfish, and the Gower used to have them by the million. Unfortunately, the beaches have been ravaged by commercial cockling and now produce a shadow of their former bounty. Randolph taught me how to riddle with a sieve and rake and we found a bucketful, of which he lovingly returned at least half to grow on. The rest, cooked on the tailgate of the Izuzu with a little local cider and cream, were a revelation, and I salute him.

Let's talk river fishing for a minute. I love fishing, and several million other Britons do as well. It seems to be part of our national psyche. There is something so deep-down exciting about outwitting a fish, whether it is with a dry fly or a maggot. But from an eating point of view it is usually the fly-fisherman who eats what he catches. Our lakes and rivers are carefully

stewarded to ensure abundant insect life and water quality, and managed to prevent overfishing. I am, at heart, a fly-fisherman. For me, the pursuit of the salmon or trout is one of the most elegant forms of hunting. Attempting to mimic the trout's natural food, either in the nymph form, or better, in the dry-fly form, is half the battle. The other half is the skill of presenting the fly to the fish in such a way that he wants to gobble it. Remember, the fish will not expend the energy in coming for a fly unless he is sure he is going to get it, so accuracy is everything.

I have had several brilliant days filming this frustrating sport for *Countrywise*, and met some real masters of the art. Lee Cummings is one of the UK's top fly-fishermen, and lives near his beloved Lake District. We met at the lonely, windswept, but achingly beautiful Devoke Tarn, which is the highest lake in England. We fished our hearts out for one little brown trout (but what a pretty trout!) and one perch. Not much, you may think, but when we cooked them in lemon juice and foil, and watched the sunset with a hint of wood smoke in the air, all was well with the world (see page 134).

A wise man once said that God does not take from the term of a man's life time spent fishing, and I am tempted to agree with him.

I grew up literally surrounded by shooting. The part of Berkshire that was my home in childhood (and still is) is very rural, and every farm and estate in the region has a shoot. Shooting has been one of the most important factors in shaping our country-side for the last 1,000 years. Almost every piece of private land in the UK (and that is most of it) provides a venue for sport shooting. Whether you agree with it or not, shoot-ing (by which I mean the formal or informal shooting of pheasants, partridges and ducks that have been reared and released for the purpose) is key to the management of the British countryside today. The fact that people pay a lot of money to come and shoot throughout the winter is a godsend to the farmers and estates in ru-ral parts of the country. The money from shooting does not go to increase the wealth of landowners, as is often said. In reality, very few shoots make money, they just plough it back into management – paying for the gamekeepers and the feed merchants and keeping the rural economy going. The simple truth is that most 'shooting folk' are by their nature committed conservationists.

'A wise man once said that God does not take from the term of a man's life time spent fishing, and I am tempted to agree with him.'

Shooting involves the careful use of the ground, which ensures a haven for wildlife and keeps the balance of the countryside in place. The important thing to me is that all game that is shot must be eaten and used. Game is healthy, with no cholesterol and very little fat; it offers good value for money and it is not imported. It has also had a really great life, being properly free range and slowly grown (in the case of pheasants and partridges). If you have not tried eating it, please buy some the next time you're in the supermarket or farmer's market and it is in season (think Autumn and Winter, on the whole).

Reared game aside, the wild game of the UK, is amazing, and is in great demand. Rabbits, pigeons and wild venison-meat that would have all have gone to France and Spain, is now mostly consumed here. It's incredible to think that on this crowded island we have no fewer than six species of wild deer, which have no natural predator apart from us. They are present in huge numbers, and those numbers are growing. Unless they're controlled, they will suffer, so you should feel no qualms about eating this most magnificent meat.

Scotland is the homeland of the deer, and it is full of them. However, red deer in Scotland are generally well managed and provide not only a large source of domestic venison, but also generate huge amounts of revenue that goes directly to the upkeep of the rural estates. This revenue comes from the large sums that people will pay to stalk the deer in the wild Scottish mountains – a truly amazing experience that is gaining in popularity.

'Game is healthy, with no cholesterol and very little fat; it offers good value for money and it is not imported.'

I was lucky enough to film *Countrywise* in the beautiful Trossachs region of Scotland with Paul Kent and Angus Churchill, two experienced stalkers who look after the red and roe deer over an area of about 30,000 acres. Spending a day with such quiet, honourable men was a real pleasure and, while the weather ruined our stalk, I learned much and will return. Paul was a fine advertisement for living on venison – tall and very fit, he has a reputation for being able to walk for days up vertical hillsides with no apparent effort.

I mainly stalk and manage the lowland species of deer. Venison is so popular in both my pubs (The Harwood Arms in London, which I co-own, as well as The Pot Kiln in Berkshire) that between the two we use about 400 deer a year. In order to fulfil that demand, I manage about 20,000 acres of private land in and around Berkshire. It works well, because everyone benefits – the farmers get their crops protected, the estates get a revenue, and I get the venison.

One of the oldest and most challenging forms of shooting to be found in the British Isles is wildfowling. It has always been, and still is, enjoyed by an eclectic bunch of individual men and women who don't mind braving waist-deep freezing-cold tidal mud flats, extremes of temperature, and ultimate discomfort, to outwit and shoot a few wily wild ducks and geese. This is surely one of the most rewarding forms of shooting. The Heacham Wildfowlers' Club has been looking after a large part of the north Norfolk coast for several decades. They have steadily improved the habitat and generally done wonders for the conservation in the area. In return for all their hard work, every year each member is allowed to shoot a few geese and ducks.

Darren, who took me out for *Countrywise*, is a master of the sport, and taught me a lot in the short time we spent together. It is astonishing how difficult it is, especially hitting the teal that come in early morning and late evening. These ducks fly spectacularly quickly and plunge down to feed from a height, like a swooping peregrine. We were lucky enough to shoot three the morning we spent crouching in the reeds, and since the weather was particularly brisk, they had cooled down by the time the sun was risen and we decided to eat.

'The recipes in this book are all simple. They have to be, or they would take too long to film. If you cannot find an ingredient, you can substitute something else. They usually offer good value for money, since I am a great proponent of using cheaper cuts of meat wherever possible.'

Filming for *Countrywise* and *Countrywise Kitchen* presents its own problems. The weather is one. I love being outdoors in foul weather but sometimes it is truly awful. This does not really matter, of course, but cooking on a barbecue in a howling gale is novel and quite tricky. One of the best things about the programme for me is the challenge of cooking a recipe on the tailgate of my trusty pick-up truck. We have developed this into quite a black art and I can assure you that everything is as you see it – no cheating allowed. Some of these recipes have made it onto my pub menus, and most are to be found here.

Now to the recipes: the dishes in this book are all easy to make. They have to be, or they would take too long to film. If you cannot find an ingredient, you can substitute something else. They usually offer good value for money, since I am a great proponent of using cheaper cuts of meat, and I am aware of the economic times we live in. There is quite a lot of slow cooking in this book, so make sure you have a couple of good, heavy sauté pans in steel or iron (pans with a high side but basically frying pans) and some large saucepans. Finally, you will need a big, heavy casserole; you will use it for everything, so go invest.

Knives are the next must-have – get some good ones, and some scissors and a heavy cleaver, and learn how to keep them sharp. A good kitchen knife is the original food processor, and knife skills are key to good cookery.

I recommend everyone cultivates a relationship with a good butcher and a good fishmonger. Once you get on well, he or she will help you source things, since repeat business is really hard to get these days. I work with one butcher who not only supplies my meat, but also taught me everything I know about wild game and deer. If you cannot get, say, roe deer venison from a butcher, then go online. Nearly all artisan meat and fish is now available online, just try a few brands or farms until you find a product you like.

Thank you for watching *Countrywise* and *Countrywise Kitchen* and for buying this book. Our countryside is so precious, and the only way we can protect it is by furthering the understanding of how it works. I am proud to be a part of such a good show and hope that you carry on enjoying it for years to come.

MEAT

MEAT

As one of the country's most ardent carnivores, I could talk for days on this subject alone. But since this book is not just about meat I will confine myself to a few thoughts. I believe that we in Britain produce the best meat in the world. There is a real resurgence in our native breeds, and we are getting away from the post-war mentality of growing meat fast by any means.

Let us start with what we are best known for: beef. We are blessed with a profusion of wonderful breeds of cattle in these islands, and during my journey with *Countrywise* I have seen quite a few of them. I have admired and tasted the best Britain has to offer, from the Sussex, to the Ruby Red Devon, to the Welsh Black, to the Highland. All the breeds have their good points, but what I really appreciate is when cattle are farmed in the area they were bred to live in. As one farmer said to me, they are of the landscape.

All these breeds give meat with slightly different qualities, depending particularly on what they eat and what their environment is. The most important considerations for me are that they are allowed to grow slowly and, once slaughtered, are then allowed to hang properly.

Hanging is key to good beef. Assuming a carcass has good conformation (that is, the right quantity of muscle and fat) it will taste fine so long as a proportion of the moisture is allowed to disappear and the meat can darken, relax and dry out a little. Only dry-aged beef will offer that. Alan Hayward, who is my mentor and a genius butcher, says that he recommends hanging the forequarters of a body of beef for up to 15 days, and the hindquarters (where all the posh cuts are) for about 30 days. This will give the meat that famous, rich, beefy flavour that shouts quality. This, combined with the farmer's hard work, will give you stellar results.

Remember that there is more to a body of beef than its fillets and sirloin. The lesser, cheaper cuts are from muscles that have done a lot of work over the years and, while they need slow cooking, they will have a fabulous flavour.

Veal is much misunderstood in the UK. I am not talking about Dutch veal that has been kept in crates and denied light and solid food. I am talking about British rose veal. These calves would have been shot at birth to keep the cows milking if they were not used for veal, but instead they are brought on for eight months before slaughter, enjoying a good standard of living. English veal is a fabulous meat, pink in colour and quite delicious, and needs to be supported as an industry. Anyone who is happy to eat lamb should have no problems with veal.

The flavour of lamb varies immensely, depending on its breed and where it's from. It is now easy to buy many varieties of lamb, from Poll Dorsets (my great friend Tom Brown farms these just up the road from me, near Reading, and they are a wonderful breed – not particularly big, but they taste fabulous) to Soay sheep from the wild islands off Scotland, which are dark and strong in flavour, to Jacobs and, of course, the now-legendary Herdwicks from the Lake District. All have one thing in common – a great life spent outdoors and some passionate people farming them.

Look for lamb that has lived to at least six months old. Very young lamb is pale and has little flavour. You should choose lamb that has a good 5mm/¼-inch of fat on its back and looks muscular. Lamb should not be hung for too long – a week is more than enough.

Mutton, once wildly out of fashion, is now popular. Strictly speaking, it is the meat from a sheep that was slaughtered at two years of age or older. Mutton is darker, stronger in flavour and larger than lamb, but the same cooking principles apply. The recipe for slow-braised shoulder of mutton on page 36 is particularly good.

What a noble animal the pig is. Once upon a time every family would have kept a pig over the summer, which would then have fed them over the Winter. Just think what the pig gives us – bacon (glorious bacon!), chops, roasts, sausages, black pudding, trotters... the list is endless. As with cattle and sheep, there is an amazing variety of pig breeds. I have a particular fondness for the Black Berkshire, with its squashed face and glorious high fat content. Other notable breeds are the Saddleback, the Oxford Sandy Black, the Tamworth and the Gloucester Old Spot. When buying pork, look for a really good layer of white fat over the meat. When purchasing chops, I like about 2cm/¾ inch of fat on them – yum.

MUSTARD-SPICED T-BONE STEAK

Serves 2   *All year round*

Beef is an evocative subject to the British; we are proud of our 'heritage cattle', and rightly so. No cow is more 'heritage' than the Sussex cow – these animals were roaming the Sussex hills when the Normans invaded in 1066, and have changed little since. Like many of our native breeds, they are perfectly adapted to their environment, having dark, curly coats that defy the Summer sun as well as the ability to graze on poor-quality Winter grass. They are 'slow-growing' animals and this was a dirty phrase for many years, but now slow-grown meat is, thank God, fashionable again.

Whatever the breed, I think the most noble cut of beef is the T-bone. It must be cut thick, at least 2.5cm/1 inch (preferably 4cm/1½ inches), and should encompass both the sirloin and the fillet. A T-bone cut like this will weigh 800–900g/1¾lb–2lb, and will set you back the best part of £20. Think of it this way: that's a tenner a head to have a massive two-person feast of the finest aged beef that Britain has to offer.

1 x 800–900g/1¾lb–2lb T-bone steak
1 tsp English mustard powder
1 tbsp vegetable oil
sea salt and freshly ground black pepper

Preheat the oven to 200°C/400°F/gas mark 6. Liberally sprinkle the meat with salt, pepper and English mustard powder. Rub the seasoning into the meat, then lightly oil a very heavy pan. Bring the pan up to heat so that the air above the pan is shimmering and the oil is smoking lightly. Drop in the T-bone and cook without moving it around for 90 seconds. Turn the steak over and cook it for another 90 seconds. Transfer the meat to a roasting tray and place it in the oven for 7 minutes for medium-rare, 8–9 minutes for medium and 10–11 minutes for well done (the cooking time will vary depending on the thickness of the steak, so do keep an eye on it). Remove it from the oven and allow it to rest on a wooden board for 10 minutes.

I like to serve a T-bone with piles of chips or crunchy, garlicky fried potatoes (see page 181) and perhaps a thin slice of butter slowly melting over the top.

BARBECUED SPICED SKEWERS OF BEEF WITH TOMATO, PARSLEY AND MINT SALAD

Serves 4   *Summer*

South Devon, particularly the area between Plymouth and Dartmouth, is a land of tall hedges, narrow lanes and verdant green fields, all overlooking a coastline of breathtaking beauty. It is also the home to Tim Jakins and family, who have been farming 500 acres of this paradise for the last 15 years.

I made this dish with their Ruby Red meat. Like many native British breeds of cattle, the Ruby Reds look at home in their landscape; they can live outdoors for most of the year and grow slowly on the rich diet of green Devon grass. These docile cattle are a magnificent reddish-chocolate colour and have an impressive marbling of fat running through the meat. The beef is as good as any I have ever tried. This recipe is ideal for the barbecue.

4 x 250g/9oz rump steaks, each cut
   2.5cm/1 inch thick
1 tsp paprika
1 tsp each ground cinnamon, ginger,
   cumin and coriander
3 tbsp natural yogurt
sea salt and freshly ground black pepper

For the salad
200g/7oz ripe cherry tomatoes, halved
1 large bunch each of flat-leaf parsley
   and mint, leaves picked
1 red chilli (chile), finely chopped
2 large banana shallots, finely sliced
100ml/3½fl oz/scant ½ cup
   extra virgin olive oil
1 clove of garlic, peeled and finely sliced
juice of 1 lemon

Cut the steaks into 2.5-cm/1-inch-square chunks. Put them in a mixing bowl, add the spices, yogurt, salt and pepper and mix well. Cover and leave to marinate in the fridge for at least 30 minutes.

Thread the meat on long metal skewers. Preheat the barbecue – if using gas, make sure the heat is medium-high (not too high); if using charcoal, make sure you don't cook until all you have are grey coals at the bottom of the barbecue. Lay the skewers over the barbecue. The beef needs to cook for 5–6 minutes on each side.

Meanwhile, work on your salad. Throw the tomatoes into a bowl. Add the parsley leaves whole, but chop up the mint. Add the chilli (check it's not too hot before you add the lot!) and shallots – raw shallots add a wonderful crunch to a salad. Pour over the oil, mix in the garlic, squeeze in the lemon juice and season with salt and pepper.

Once the skewers are cooked, remove from the heat and leave to rest for 5 minutes. Pull the meat off the skewers, pile it on the plates, spoon the salad on the side, and serve with the flatbreads on page 223. Open a bottle of rosé and soak up the sun.

BEEF SHIN AND OXTAIL SUET PUDDING

Serves 6   *Autumn/Winter*

I made this dish with meat from the Welsh Black cattle of the Gower Peninsula. It's wonderful to see these stately animals feeding in the sand dunes and marshlands along the seashores of this magnificent coastline – and they taste as good as they look.

Most of us are familiar with rib-eye, sirloin and rump, but not everybody has used the traditionally chewier cuts of beef such as shin, blade and oxtail. I love cooking with this 'poor man's beef', because these cuts represent great value for money and, once cooked for a long time, always taste magnificent.

For this recipe we are going to use the shin and the tail of the beast, cooked with beer, in a suet pastry, to produce the richest, heartiest savoury British pudding ever!

For the pastry
400g/14oz/2⅔ cups plain (all-purpose) flour, plus extra for dusting
300g/11oz shredded beef suet
a pinch of salt
approx 200ml/7fl oz/scant 1 cup cold water
butter, to grease

For the filling
1 tbsp vegetable oil
2 tbsp plain (all-purpose) flour, seasoned

1.5kg/3lb 5oz beef oxtail on the bone
1kg/2¼lb diced shin of beef, well trimmed and cut into 2.5cm/1-inch dice
2 large onions, peeled and finely sliced
1 tbsp tomato purée (paste)
2 large field mushrooms, quartered
2 litres/3½ pints/2 quarts strong bitter beer (you may not need all of this)
freshly ground black pepper

To make the pastry, mix the flour, suet and salt together in a bowl. Add enough cold water to create a firm but pliable dough. Wrap in clingfilm (plastic wrap) and leave to rest in the fridge.

For the filling, heat the oil in a large frying pan over a medium heat. On a plate, lightly flour the oxtail, and fry until golden brown on both sides. Remove from the pan and set aside. Repeat with the shin, then remove from the pan and set aside. Add the onions, tomato purée (paste) and mushrooms to the pan and fry until golden.

Tip both meats, the onions and mushrooms into a large flameproof casserole and pour in enough beer to cover the meat. Grind in plenty of black pepper, then cover and cook over a low heat for 3 hours. Leave to cool. Remove the meat and vegetables and set aside in a bowl. Pick the oxtail meat from the bone in chunks. If necessary, leave the remaining liquid over the heat, uncovered, to reduce; it should be dark and thick. Cover and set aside.

continues overleaf >

Roll out two-thirds of the pastry on a lightly floured surface to 5mm/¼ inch thick, then use it to line a well-greased 1.1-litre/2-pint pudding basin (heatproof bowl). Roll out the remaining pastry to a circle large enough to use as a lid. Spoon the meat and onion mixture into the pastry-lined basin. Pour in 2 ladles of braising liquid and place the pastry lid on top. Dampen the edges and crimp shut. Add a greaseproof (wax) paper lid and tie it on with string. Put the pudding basin into a large pan, add 5cm/2 inches of hot water to the pan, cover and steam for 3 hours. Turn the pudding upside down on to a serving plate… a magnificent suet pudding will be revealed. Reheat any remaining gravy and pour over the top.

VEAL CHOP WITH MADEIRA AND MORELS

Serves 4   *Spring/Summer*

I cooked this little dish on the tailgate of the Isuzu on a beautiful farm overlooking Morecambe Bay. The recipe is a French classic, but I know of no more sumptuous flavour combination than good veal, fabulous morel mushrooms and Madeira. Served with lashings of mashed potatoes, this is just sensational – and dead easy to make. Proper dinner party fare.

50g/2oz/¼ cup butter, plus extra
4 x 200g/7oz veal chops
50g/2oz bacon lardons, finely chopped
24 baby onions, peeled and finely chopped
2 sprigs of thyme, leaves picked
125ml/4fl oz/½ cup of Madeira

125ml/4fl oz/½ cup red wine
200ml/7fl oz/scant 1 cup of chicken stock
50g/2oz morels, soaked in hot water for 15 minutes
1 tbsp plain (all-purpose) flour
sea salt and freshly ground black pepper

Put a heavy pan over a medium–high heat and drop in the butter. Season the chops with salt and pepper and brown them in the pan for 2 minutes on each side. Remove the chops and set them aside. Add the bacon and baby onions to the pan and cook for 3–4 minutes, then add the thyme leaves and cook for a further 5 minutes to caramelize the onions. Deglaze the pan with the Madeira, then add the wine and stock and cook for 5 minutes. Add the morels and a splash of the morel liquor and continue to cook until the liquor has reduced to a thick consistency; about 5 minutes.

Return the chops to the pan and cook them for 3 minutes or until cooked, spooning the juice over them the whole time. Remove the chops and put them aside to rest. Continue to cook the sauce until it has reduced to the desired consistency. To finish the sauce, rub a couple of small knobs of butter into the flour, then stir in until dissolved. Serve the chop in the sauce with seriously rich mash.

BEEF SHORT RIBS BRAISED IN STOUT AND ONIONS

Serves 6   *All year round*

Short ribs are otherwise known as Jacob's ribs and comprise the central 15cm/6 inches or so of the ribs of a body of beef. To my mind, short ribs are the ultimate beef cut in terms of flavour and cheapness. The downside is that there is no way to make them look attractive; they will always look like a big lump of meat attached to a bone. Think of them as beefy lamb shanks and you won't go far wrong.

Because the muscles between the ribs work so hard, the meat is both tough and fatty. This, of course, makes it a prime candidate for very slow cooking, which will get rid of most of the fat and tenderize the meat.

Stout and onions really work well in this dish – the slight bitterness of the beer counteracts the sweet fattiness of the meat. This dish is best served in a deep bowl, piled high with buttery mashed potato.

50ml/2fl oz/scant ¼ cup vegetable oil
6 tbsp plain (all-purpose) flour
1 tbsp English mustard powder
6 short ribs of beef
4 large onions, peeled and finely sliced
6 cloves of garlic, unpeeled

1 small bunch of thyme, tied with string
1 tbsp tomato purée (paste)
500ml/17fl oz/2 cups beef stock
1 litre/1¾ pints/2 pints (US) dark stout
a couple of knobs of butter (optional)
sea salt and freshly ground black pepper

Heat the oil in a large, deep casserole over a medium-high heat. Mix the flour and mustard powder together and roll the short ribs in it. Place the ribs in the hot oil and brown them well on all sides. Remove the meat from the pan and put to one side. Reduce the heat to medium.

Preheat the oven to 100°C/200°F/gas mark ⅛. Add the onions to the pan, then cook for 20 minutes or so until they are really brown. Add the garlic, thyme and tomato purée and mix well. Pour in the beef stock and stout. Nestle the short ribs back into the pot – they should be covered in liquid or nearly so. Place a lid on the pot and cook in the oven overnight, or for at least 8 hours, until cooked and tender.

The next morning, remove the short ribs from the liquor and carefully remove the layer of fat from the top. Taste the remaining gravy and season if necessary. Thicken, if need be, by stirring a couple of knobs of butter rolled in flour into the liquor on a medium heat. Put the ribs back in for a final warming. Serve on mash.

THE PERFECT BURGER

Serves 4-6 *All year round*

When we filmed this recipe for *Countrywise Kitchen*, I found some particularly good beef mince. Use the mince from the shoulder of the animal, and make sure that the butcher includes a good amount of fat in the mix. The key to a good burger is to make the flavours you add to the meat complementary – they do not want to clash. The meat has to be properly seasoned and not overcooked. Finally, the burger has to be big! I like to make these babies about 275g/10oz in weight. A good tip is to measure out the mixture for each burger in a large coffee mug, then form the burger between your hands. This way you get the same amount every time.

For the burgers

1kg/2¼lb prime beef mince (ground beef) with a good bit of fat in it
1 tbsp finely chopped parsley
1 tbsp finely chopped oregano
1 tbsp finely chopped thyme
2 shallots, finely chopped
2 handfuls of breadcrumbs, ideally Panko (see page 46)
1 tbsp wholegrain mustard
1 tbsp sea salt
1 tsp freshly ground black pepper
2 tbsp tomato ketchup
1 tbsp Worcestershire sauce

To finish

1 tbsp vegetable oil
4–6 slices of mature Cheddar
8–12 slices of smoked streaky bacon
4–6 burger buns
tomato ketchup
Celeriac remoulade (see page 191)
green salad leaves, dressed

The day before your barbecue (or at least 4 hours before), mix all the burger ingredients together in a big bowl using your hands. Cover and put in the fridge.

Preheat the barbecue to medium-hot (if using gas, make sure the heat is not too high; if using charcoal, make sure you don't cook until all you have are grey hot coals at the bottom of the barbecue).

Form the burger mixture into four huge or six smaller burgers and lightly oil them all over. Barbecue for 2–3 minutes on each side, then lay the cheese and bacon over the top of each one, lower the lid of the barbecue or cover with foil, and cook for 5 minutes more, or until the bacon is cooked through and the cheese has melted. This should cook the burgers to medium.

Toast the buns on the barbecue. Lay each burger on a bun, and accompany with ketchup, Celeriac remoulade and lovely dressed green salad leaves. Lean forward and eat with both hands – that way the grease won't run down your shirt. Drink cold beer.

ROASTED CHUMP OF SPRING LAMB WITH CHERRY TOMATOES AND GREEN BEANS

Serves 8   *Spring/Summer*

Spring lamb is a bit of a misnomer, since lamb is definitely best eaten after it has been alive for more than six months – less than that and, in my opinion, it doesn't have much flavour.

Ask your butcher to cut you the chumps. The chump is at the very end of the haunch, it is effectively the rump on a body of beef. It is a delicious cut, much underused and underrated. You can get it from any butcher, it roasts beautifully, and one chump feeds exactly two people, so you have portion control for good measure.

Look for a lamb that has a nice marbling of fat and is a good colour.

4 x 400g/7oz chumps of lamb, halved (ask your butcher to do this for you)
3 tbsp olive oil
400g/14oz cherry tomatoes on the vine
500g/1lb 2oz young fresh green (string) beans, stalks removed
10–12 cloves of garlic, unpeeled
4 anchovies

For the gremolata
zest of 2 large unwaxed lemons
1 large bunch of rosemary, leaves picked and very finely chopped
1 large bunch of flat-leaf parsley, finely chopped
4 cloves of garlic, peeled and grated
4 tbsp extra-virgin olive oil
sea salt and freshly ground black pepper

Start by making the gremolata (the piquant marinade that we are going to cook our chumps in). Put the lemon zest, rosemary, parsley, garlic and oil into a bowl and season with a generous sprinkling of sea salt and a lot of black pepper. Mix well.

Put half the gremolata in a large zip lock bag and add the chumps. Mix well in your hands, then seal and pop the bag into the fridge for 8 hours. When you are ready to cook the chumps, remove them from the bag and allow them to come up to room temperature, covered. Preheat the oven to 200°C/400°F/gas mark 6.

Get a heavy pan up to a high heat, then sear the lamb so it is golden all over. Take the lamb out of the pan and sprinkle it with the second half of the gremolata. Set aside, covered. Meanwhile, add the oil to the pan and mix in the cherry tomatoes, green beans, garlic and anchovies. Pop this in the oven for 7–8 minutes. Place the lamb on top of the beans and tomatoes and return the pan to the oven for a further 9–10 minutes, or until the lamb is cooked. Remove from the oven and allow the lamb to rest for 10–15 minutes. To serve, carve the juicy lamb. Spoon the green beans and cherry tomatoes into four deep bowls, top with the lamb and then with the gremolata.

SLOW-BRAISED SHOULDER OF MUTTON

Serves 4–6   *Autumn/Winter*

Mutton has long lapsed in popularity compared to its younger cousin. This is a crying shame, for I believe well-grown mutton to be one of the finest meats produced on the British isles. While mutton may be difficult to find in your local butcher, it is widely available on the internet. For example, the wonderful Herdwick from the Lake District that I used when I cooked this recipe is strongly flavoured, as befits most highland breeds. Some lowland breeds will taste milder in comparison. Whatever you choose, shoulder of mutton requires long, slow cooking to bring out the best results.

250g/9oz/1¼ cups salted butter, softened and diced

1 large bunch of oregano or rosemary, leaves picked and finely chopped

8 salted anchovies

zest of 1 unwaxed lemon

1 x approx 2.5kg/5½lb shoulder of mutton on the bone

8 banana shallots, peeled and halved lengthways

2 whole bulbs of garlic, peeled and halved

1 x 750ml bottle of red wine

freshly ground black pepper to taste

Preheat the oven to 140°C/275°F/gas mark 1. Put the butter in a food processor. Add the herbs, reserving a little for later, and then the anchovies, lemon zest and black pepper. Whizz to a coarse paste – about 20 seconds will do it.

Slather the paste all over the top of the mutton to a thickness of about 5mm/¼ inch. Put the shallots and garlic in a deep roasting tray and add any remaining herbs. Lay the mutton on top and pour in the wine; the liquid should just be touching the bottom of the meat – if not, top up with water.

Seal the top of the roasting tray with a layer of baking parchment followed by foil. Place the tray in the oven for at least 6 hours (overnight at 100°C/200°F/gas mark ⅛ works too), or until the mutton is cooked.

Remove the foil and baking parchment and turn the heat up to 200°C/400°F/gas mark 6 to crisp up the crust for 20 minutes. Strain the juices, discarding the garlic and shallots, reduce a little in a saucepan, uncovered, over a medium heat, season and set aside to use as a gravy.

This is lovely served with braised red cabbage and mustard mashed potatoes.

OVERNIGHT LEG OF LAMB WITH RATATOUILLE AND GARLIC TOASTS

Serves 12   *Summer*

I am very lucky to live in a place where there are some fantastic ingredients within spitting distance. One of my favourite, and indeed one of my customers' favourite, ingredients is to be found on my friend Tom Brown's farm. Tom rears a flock of beautiful Poll Dorset lambs. This is a wonderful breed; the sheep are not particularly big, have a fabulous flavour and live outdoors (I know Tom's live outdoors because I drive past them every day), and every year I am lucky enough to get the pick of the lambs.

Lamb legs are quite tricky to cook. You must decide if you are going to cook yours slowly or quickly. If you want it pink, you have to cook it fairly quickly. If you like it falling off the bone, Continental-style, you have to cook it very slowly and lovingly. I infinitely prefer the slow-cooked way. One of the joys of lamb (and mutton) is its fattiness; you can cook it for a long time, it doesn't dry out, and it has a juiciness that makes your mouth water.

We are going to cook our leg of lamb in a style that is reminiscent of southern France. This is a one-pot dish. It is my idea of heaven and doesn't half keep the amount of washing up down. Also, of course, the beauty of cooking in one pot is that you retain flavour and the vegetables will be infused with a glorious lambiness. With herbs galore and tons of garlic, it's a dish that packs a powerful punch.

4 red onions, peeled, and each cut into 4 pieces
12 banana shallots, peeled
6 whole bulbs of garlic, unpeeled
4 sticks (stalks) of celery, cut into smallish pieces
3 large courgettes (zucchini), sliced into rounds
3 red (bell) peppers, deseeded and cut
    into largish chunks
150ml/5fl oz/scant ⅔ cup extra-virgin
    olive oil, plus extra for the garlic toast
500g/1lb 2oz cherry tomatoes
1 very large bunch of rosemary
2 x 1.5kg/3lb 5oz legs of lamb
    (alternatively, you could use shoulder)
1 litre/1¾ pints/4½ cups lamb or chicken stock
1 x 750ml bottle of red wine
slices of crusty white bread
sea salt and freshly ground black pepper

The great thing about one-pot cooking is that the method is usually incredibly simple. For this recipe you will require the largest, most heroic casserole dish that you can lay your hands on. I have a huge orange Le Creuset casserole dish that I have had for years; it will take two legs of lamb and feed a dozen people. If you don't own one, go and buy one: you will never regret it.

Preheat the oven to 120°C/250°F/gas mark ½. Put the red onions and shallots into the casserole. Put the bulbs of garlic in whole and untouched. Add the celery, courgettes and peppers, pour in the oil, add the tomatoes and stir well.

Make a bundle out of the rosemary and tie it up with string, then add it to the casserole. Nestle the lamb into the mixture, pushing it down. Pour in the stock and red wine. Bring to a simmer on the hob.

Grind plenty of black pepper into the casserole, then pop the lid on and place it in the oven for 12 hours. Check after 4–5 hours – if it is bubbling, turn the heat down to 90–100°C/190–200°F/gas mark ⅛, or as low as your oven will go. Check every hour or so to make sure the mixture is not bubbling dry; if it is, add more red wine.

When you are ready to eat, take the casserole out of the oven and gingerly remove the legs of lamb, which will be falling apart. With extreme care, lay them on a large wooden chopping board and let them rest.

Now check the mixture remaining in the casserole. You should have a gloriously thick, ratatouille-like affair in the bottom of the dish. Check the seasoning, and if necessary add salt, then remove the bulbs of garlic. Allow the bulbs to cool for 5 minutes, then squeeze their contents into a bowl. Drizzle some crusty white bread with olive oil, spread the garlic paste over the bread and toast in the oven for 5 minutes, until crispy.

Give each person a slice of toast, spoon the ratatouille over it and then pull large, fragrant, steaming lumps of beautifully tender lamb off the bone and lay alongside the vegetables. You will almost certainly need to open another bottle of red wine to accompany this dish!

ROAST LOIN OF PORK WITH CRACKLING AND CARROTS BRAISED IN CIDER

Serves 6   *All year round*

Perfect roast pork requires perfect crackling – a fact about which all of us would agree. As most of us would attest to, however, reaching this goal can be tricky. First we have to start with the raw ingredient. There are many breeds of pig in the British Isles, from the Black Berkshire to the Gloucester Old Spot to the Oxford Sandy and Black, and proponents of each will argue their merits. A couple of factors are crucial to any really good piece of roast pork. Firstly, the pig must have had a good, well-fed, outdoor life. Secondly, it must have a decent layer of fat between the skin and meat. Size-zero pigs do not crackle well!

For this recipe I used a loin of Gloucester Old Spot with a solid 2cm/¾ inch layer of fat – lovely. This fat will keep the meat moist and juicy during cooking and help the skin crackle to perfection.

1 x 1.5kg/3lb 5oz 6-rib loin of pork,
    French-trimmed, with chine bone
    removed but retained
2 tbsp honey
2 tbsp wholegrain mustard
12 medium carrots
1 litre/1¾ pints/4½ cups cider
sea salt and freshly ground black pepper

Preheat the oven to 220°C/425°F/gas mark 7. Remove the skin from the pork. Mix the honey and mustard together. Season the loin with salt and pepper, then smear the honey and mustard mixture over it. Put the skin back on the loin.

Place the loin on the chine bone. Re-attach everything with string between each exposed rib. Sit the loin upright in a roasting tin (pan).

Nestle the carrots all around and pour in the cider, then sprinkle salt over the skin.

Roast for 45 minutes. Turn the heat down to 160°C/325°F/gas mark 3 and roast for a further 45 minutes, or until cooked through, topping up with more cider if necessary. Remove from the oven and leave to rest for 20 minutes. Cut the string and portion the crackling.

Throw away the chine bone and cut between each rib for perfect chops. Serve with the glazed carrots.

SLOW-COOKED ROLLED BELLY OF PORK WITH OREGANO AND GARLIC

Serves 12   *All year round*

Pork belly has become immensely popular in recent years. This is probably due to the incredible value for money it offers. The downside of pork belly is that, unless cooked slowly, it is tough and chewy, and there is a considerable amount of fat involved. When slow-cooked for a really long time at a very low temperature it almost confits itself; in other words it cooks itself in its own fat. This is a fantastic and admirable trait, because it leaves amazingly juicy meat that falls apart, and I think this is the reason for its huge popularity in gastropubs and restaurants in recent years.

This recipe is what we call bombproof. In other words, it never goes wrong if you follow the simple instructions. When buying the meat, make sure you buy a good-quality large pork belly with a reasonably thick layer of fat – the fat will disappear during cooking, leaving the meat gloriously juicy. Ask the butcher to remove the bones between the ribs and thus leave you with a boneless pork belly.

1 x 2.5kg/5½lb pork belly, rib bones removed
1 very large bunch of oregano
1 small bunch of rosemary
12 cloves of garlic, peeled and
   coarsely chopped
zest of 1 unwaxed lemon
150ml/5fl oz/scant ⅔ cup extra-virgin olive oil
10 large banana shallots or red onions,
   peeled and halved
1.7 litres/3 pints/7½ cups dry cider
sea salt and freshly ground black pepper

To cook this dish you must invest in some good-quality butchers' string, which can be bought from any butcher. A roll should not cost you more than £5 and should last you forever. Do not use string that could melt (anybody seen *Bridget Jones's Diary*?!), because this will lead to embarrassing consequences and a failed dish.

Preheat the oven to 200°C/400°F/gas mark 6. Score the skin of the pork belly with a good knife. Lay the pork out, skin-side down, and rub the flesh with salt and pepper, in reasonably generous quantities.

Throw the herb leaves into a food processor. Add the garlic and lemon zest and pour in the oil. Whizz the mixture until you have a fairly fine paste. Smear handfuls of this paste all over the flesh of the pork, making sure it gets into every nook and cranny.

It's time to tie the belly with the butchers' string. We are tying to create a long cylinder of meat, tied from side to side. The best way to do this is to start by tying both ends with string (and also a loop in the middle to help secure it), then work your way from one end to another, making sure the string is reasonably tight and evenly spaced, about 2.5cm/1 inch apart. You may wish to cut the narrow, fatty end off the pork belly, as this will make it more even.

Find your largest roasting dish. Lay the shallots or onions in the bottom of it. Add the cider, which should come just level with the top of the shallots. Nestle the rolled belly of pork on top, making sure that the cider is just below the level of the pork. Rub the top of the skin with more salt. Roast for 1 hour.

Turn the oven down to 100°C/200°F/gas mark ⅛ and cook for 4–6 hours (if you cook it overnight at this temperature it will not come to any harm). Remove from the oven – if it is not crispy enough, turn the oven up to maximum for the last half hour of cooking. You should have an incredibly crisp outer layer of crackling with perfect circular indentations from the string.

Carve between the strings and lay perfect rounds of super-crispy pork belly on the plate. Served with braised red cabbage, roasted potatoes and all the trimmings, this makes a fabulous Sunday lunch. If you haven't cooked it at too high a heat, you should also have lovely cidery juice at the bottom of the roasting tray, which has been seasoned by the shallots and will make fantastic gravy.

STICKY SPICED PORK RIBS

Serves 4–6   *All year round*

Everywhere in the world where the pig is venerated as an eating animal,
the ribs are considered a serious delicacy – everywhere, that is, except Britain,
where we have never really got into the joys of sucking the meat off piggy
ribs. To the Americans, pork ribs on a barbecue are akin to a religion and,
of course, they are adored by the Chinese as spare ribs. The fact is that
pork ribs are incredibly cheap, really easy to cook, and brilliant for sharing
outdoors in the Summer. I like to start cooking the ribs in an oven on a low
heat and then finish them either on the barbecue or, because I can, in my
wood-fired oven.

2 thumb-sized pieces of fresh root
    ginger, grated
6 cloves of garlic, peeled and crushed
150ml/5fl oz/scant ⅔ cup dark soy sauce
75ml/2½fl oz/scant ⅓ cup maple syrup
150ml/5fl oz/scant ⅔ cup hoisin sauce
1 tsp five-spice powder
juice of 2 limes
2 x 1.3kg/2¾lb racks of pork ribs
freshly ground black pepper

Put the ginger in a medium bowl. Add the garlic, soy sauce, maple syrup, hoisin
sauce, five-spice powder, lime juice and black pepper. Mix well. Place the ribs
in a deep oven tray. Pour two-thirds of the marinade over the ribs and rub in
well. Cover and leave in the fridge for at least 4 hours.

Preheat the oven to 180°C/350°F/gas mark 4. Put the tray containing the ribs
into the oven and cook for 45 minutes, until cooked through. When you are ready
to serve, transfer the ribs to the barbecue and brush with the remaining third of
the marinade to form a glaze. Barbecue until sticky. (If you don't wish to use the
barbecue, turn your oven up to maximum for the last 10 minutes.)

Use a knife or cleaver to cut the ribs into individual pieces. Pile up in a bowl,
attack with sticky fingers, and serve lots of cold beer.

THE HARWOOD ARMS
SCOTCH EGG

Makes 6   *All year round*

It is astonishing how much fuss the humble Scotch egg has caused in the last few years. Restaurants all over the country have been falling upon it as if it were a new invention. I can tell you from experience, put them on the menu and they sell like nothing on earth.

There must be some British fascination with this combination of glorious runny egg and delicious flavoured meats and crunchy breadcrumbs. We make them at The Harwood Arms pub using the mince from our venison and herb sausage-meat to go with our beautiful free-range eggs, and they are incredibly popular.

The key to a great Scotch egg is to make sure you have terrifically well-flavoured meat, glorious crunchy breadcrumbs (use Panko – they are used in Japanese cooking and absorb less oil than ordinary breadcrumbs, so produce a good crunchy texture when fried) and, most importantly, a gorgeous vivid-yellow, free-range runny egg yolk in the middle. When the Scotch egg is cut open, you get a delicious gooeyness right through the centre. Timing is the key. They aren't hard to make; just follow these simple steps.

6 eggs, at room temperature
400g/14oz/generous 1⅔ cups
    (ground) pork sausagemeat, or
    50% pork and 50% beef
400g/14oz/generous 3½ cups
    (ground) venison mince
1 small bunch of thyme, leaves picked
    and finely chopped
1 tbsp wholegrain mustard
100g/3½oz/⅔ cup plain
    (all-purpose) flour
3 eggs, beaten, for eggwash
250g/9oz/2 cups Panko breadcrumbs
    (see introduction)
vegetable oil, for deep-frying
cornichons (baby gherkins) to serve
sea salt and freshly ground black pepper

Boil the six eggs in just-boiling water for exactly 5 minutes. Depending on at what altitude you are (atmospheric pressure plays a large part in accurate times for boiling eggs), you might have to adjust this figure by a few seconds. As soon as the time is up, plunge the eggs into iced water to cool. Ideally, once the eggs have been cooled you should be able to peel them. The whites should be firm, but should enclose a very runny centre.

Mix the two types of meat together in a bowl. Add the thyme, mustard, salt and pepper and mix well.

Put the flour in a shallow bowl. With wet hands, take a piece of sausagemeat that is the same size as the peeled egg and flatten it out in the palm of your hand, until it is approximately 5mm/¼ inch thick. Lightly flour the peeled egg and lay it in the centre of the sausagemeat. Continually wetting your hands, wrap the egg in the sausagemeat and smooth well to ensure there are no gaps. This will give you a perfect meat-bound egg. Set aside and continue like this until all six eggs are ready.

Put the beaten eggs in a shallow bowl and the breadcrumbs in a second shallow bowl. Roll the eggs in the flour, then in the beaten eggs and then in the breadcrumbs. If you wish, repeat with the beaten eggs and breadcrumbs for a thicker armour. Place the breadcrumbed eggs in the fridge, covered.

When you are ready to cook your Scotch eggs (and, indeed, these should always be cooked to order), deep-fry at 180°C/350°F in clean vegetable oil for 5½ minutes until golden brown.

Serve with a sprinkling of sea salt on top and a handful of cornichons to one side, to cut through the fatty meat. Ideally, a pint of proper ale should be drunk with this national dish.

DEER, RABBIT AND HARE

DEER, RABBIT AND HARE

I believe that deer are a huge asset to Britain and should not be taken for granted. They give us what is arguably the world's healthiest meat, which is low in cholesterol, high in antioxidants, and has no saturated fat. Venison is essentially a superfood, which has had the best possible life and a very humane death. Who could ask for more? The fact that deer are so beautiful is a problem for most people, so I would say, think with your head and not your heart. If you want to eat healthily, ethically, and cheaply, then go for venison. It is increasingly available in supermarkets (usually farmed red deer). For wild venison, go online or to farmers' markets, and get the species you want.

There are, astonishingly, six species of deer in the wild in the UK. From smallest to biggest they are: muntjac, Chinese water, roe, sika, fallow and red.

The muntjac is a much-maligned little creature. From its introduction from Malaysia to Britain at Woburn Abbey at the turn of the 20th century, it has done staggeringly well, adapting to the southern British climate as though it were native to these shores. It is a highly unusual deer in that it does not have a set breeding season, but produces an offspring every seven months, regardless of the time of year, which is why there is no closed season for shooting them. This, added to the fact that it is generally lower than the height of the undergrowth it dwells in and has a propensity for living in people's gardens, makes it a very difficult animal to control, and numbers are going through the roof. Their qualities as food are amazing: they taste a bit like lamb, with firm meat that is very fine in grain.

Chinese water deer are another introduction; they do well in East Anglia, but have not migrated elsewhere. They make delicious meat, with a thick layer of fat over their backs and tasting more like lamb than venison.

Roe deer is one of our native breeds. Nearly hunted to extinction in the 17th century, the roe is coming back in huge numbers all over the country. The most lovely, graceful animals on earth (in my view), roe deer adapt well to living near people, many spending their whole lives in domestic gardens. Their qualities as food are excellent – they are considered the Rolls Royce of venison, giving soft, mild, tender meat that is very easy to cook.

Sika venison is nothing short of amazing. I think it is probably the best. The meat is firm, dark and delicious. Large populations exist in Scotland, Ireland and Dorset.

The fallow is the deer I stalk and cook most often. The meat is brilliant – grainy, not too strong and yields well. If I had to choose one species to shoot and cook, this would be it. This and roe are the ones to ask your butcher for.

Our most noble wild animal, the red deer used to be found throughout Britain, but is now restricted to Scotland, East Anglia and the South-West. The meat is dark and can be delicious, so long as it is not hung for too long. This is the most prolific source of venison in the UK, and the meat you are most likely to find in the supermarket. It is also the species that is most often farmed.

There is no fat in venison, so to keep it juicy you must not overcook it, and you must rest it properly after cooking. These beasts are athletes, and if you don't rest the meat, the muscle fibres will contract and squeeze out the juices.

Rabbits have lived in Britain since Roman times, when they were an important source of food. From then until the 1950s, country folk relied on them as valuable protein. Then Myxomatosis struck and reduced the population by 95 per cent in a few months. In the years since then the bunny has made a comeback and they are now causing an agricultural problem once again.

From a cook's point of view rabbits are great – healthy and, if shot right (I think a culinary rabbit should always be shot in the head with a rifle, not a shotgun) very mild in flavour. Gut and hang rabbits immediately, and cook them within 72 hours to ensure mildness. You should confit or slow-cook older rabbits, but young three-quarter grown beasts can be cooked quickly or made into faggots. Bear in mind that a farmed rabbit is not the same thing at all; delicious in their own right, they taste similar to chicken.

The hare is an iconic British mammal. Recipes using brown hare are some of the earliest to have been written down in this country. The hare was historically considered to be one of the most important animals of the chase, and thus has been heavily protected by the nobility for its own use. In post-war years, hares suffered a massive decline in numbers due to intensive agricultural activity and, in particular, the spraying of fields with noxious chemicals. Thankfully, hare numbers have risen dramatically. This is due mainly to sympathetic farming techniques – indeed, in some areas hares are now carefully managed.

BUTTERFLY-ROASTED HAUNCH OF MUNTJAC VENISON WITH GREEN SAUCE

Serves 4   *August to April*

Regarded by connoisseurs as possibly the finest venison, the muntjac should be considered as a valuable source of wild food rather than as a pest. If you can't source a haunch of muntjac, a half leg of lamb will serve as a suitable alternative for this dish.

1 x 900g/2lb haunch of muntjac
    venison, butterflied

For the marinade
100ml/3½fl oz/scant ½ cup olive oil
6 sprigs of rosemary, leaves picked
4 cloves of garlic, peeled
1 tbsp black peppercorns, crushed
1 red chilli (chile), deseeded and finely
    chopped

For the green sauce
1 clove of garlic, peeled
2 banana shallots, peeled
a handful of basil leaves
a handful of chervil
a handful of flat-leaf parsley
juice and zest of 1 unwaxed lemon
1 tbsp baby capers
2 anchovies, chopped
100ml/3½fl oz/scant ½ cup very best
    extra-virgin olive oil
sea salt and freshly ground black pepper

Put all the marinade ingredients in a food processor and whizz into a smooth paste.

To butterfly the haunch of muntjac, remove the shank of the leg through the joint, then turn the haunch over and, using a sharp knife, cut down to the thigh bone and remove it. Butterfly the leg open until it is 2.5cm/1 inch thick; if you have any problems, take it to your butcher (or come on one of my venison courses!). Place the meat in a roasting tin (pan) and pour over the marinade, making sure every bit of the meat is covered. Cover with foil and leave in the fridge for 1 hour or more.

Light your barbecue and let the flames die down until they are grey hot (or preheat a griddle pan to medium-hot). Barbecue the meat for 7 minutes either side, then rest for 14 minutes. (If cooking on a griddle pan, brown the meat for 2–3 minutes on each side, then roast in the oven for 10 minutes at 220°C/425°F/gas mark 7.) Rest for 15 minutes in a warm place.

While the meat is resting, make the green sauce. Finely chop the garlic, shallots and herbs (the finer the better). Tip them into a small bowl, add the lemon juice and zest, capers, anchovies and oil and season with salt and pepper. Carve the meat into 20–30 thin slices, cutting across the grain at a diagonal. Serve the green sauce on the side. This is delicious made into a sandwich with Moroccan flatbread (see page 223).

PAVÉ OF FALLOW DEER VENISON

Serves 4   *All year round*

The *pavé* is my favourite cut of venison. The idea for it comes from a classic French brasserie cut of beef called a *pavé de rumsteck*. Unlike a British rump of beef, the French remove the individual muscles from within the rump, trim them and cut them into cobblestone-sized chunks – hence the name *pavé*. These fabulous chunks of meat are seared, then roasted in a hot oven and usually served with chips and béarnaise sauce. Many years ago, when I lived and worked in France, this was my favourite food. At that time I was developing my passion for deer and stalking, and wondered if there was something more that one could do with a haunch of venison than roast it. This recipe was born. To prepare the *pavé*, debone the haunch, remove and separate the primal muscles and trim them of all sinew. You will be left with four fat-free, lean, odd-shaped pieces of meat that can be cut to similar-sized chunks. One haunch of medium-sized fallow will produce 16 *pavés*; in comparison, a fully grown roe deer will give 11 *pavé* per haunch.

a handful of thyme or oregano
    (thyme is my favourite herb to go
    with venison), finely chopped
1 tsp black peppercorns, crushed
1 clove of garlic, peeled and
    finely chopped

2 tbsp olive oil
4 x 175g/6oz *pavé* of fallow deer venison,
    ideally wild (ask the butcher to cut
    them for you, and see introduction)
sea salt

Mix the thyme with the crushed peppercorns, garlic and oil. Pour this into a ziplock freezer bag. Add the *pavés*, remove the excess air (I do this with a straw), then roll the bag around in your hands to ensure the meat is fully coated. Refrigerate for 2 hours. Like this, the venison will keep beautifully in the fridge for up to a week; alternatively, it can be frozen in the bag for up to 3 months; the combination of the bag and the oil-based marinade prevent freezer burn and keep the meat in perfect condition.

One hour before you wish to eat, remove the *pavés* from the fridge and allow them to come up to room temperature. Preheat the oven to 200°C/400°F/gas mark 6. Preheat a roasting tray (pan) on the hob. Take the *pavés* out of the bag and season with salt (never add salt to the marinade, or you will start to cure the venison).

Sear the *pavés* in the hot tin (pan) – it should sizzle but not scorch – for 1 minute on each side, then place the tin in the oven for 6 minutes. Take the *pavés* out of the tin, turn them over and place them on a wooden board. Leave uncovered to rest for 8 minutes – this is crucial for the proper cooking of venison (it will not go cold). Carve each *pavé* into six diaganol slices across the grain. Serve with buttery mashed potato, lightly cooked black cabbage and a thin slice of butter melting over the top.

SMOKED RACK OF FALLOW DEER

Serves 6   *August to April*

This is a stunning way of cooking a rack of wild fallow deer venison. The fallow deer (also known as dama dama) has been in Britain since Roman times, and for me is the perfect venison to eat. Treat a rack like this with respect and please don't overcook it. The idea of roasting the loin, then smoking it in hay, came from my great friend and business partner, Brett Graham, who owns the world-famous Ledbury restaurant in London's Notting Hill. I have shamelessly stolen the idea for this dish from him (with his permission, of course!). It is easy to do, requires no special equipment and adds a new depth of flavour to this most noble and delicious of meats. Ask your butcher to prepare the cut exactly as it says below.

2 tbsp black peppercorns
1 tbsp sea salt
1 bunch of fresh thyme, finely chopped
1 bunch of oregano, finely chopped
1 long-boned, French-trimmed rack of fallow deer venison
    from a 2–3-year-old animal so it is medium-sized; ask for
    the chine bone to be removed but given to you
1 tbsp extra virgin olive oil, plus extra for frying
2 large handfuls of hay (you can buy clean hay in most pet shops in Britain)

Preheat the oven to 200°C/400°F/gas mark 6. Crush the peppercorns to a coarse consistency in a pestle and mortar and mix with the sea salt. Mix in the herbs.

Remove any silvery-coloured sinew that is attached to the meat of the venison loin. Rub the oil into the meat, then spread the seasoning mixture onto a board in a line as long as the venison and roll the meat in it, ensuring it is well covered.

Preheat a large frying pan over a medium-high heat, pour in a little more oil and brown the venison all over until it is golden brown. Place the venison on its chine bone (this will protect the meat from the direct heat in the pan and ensure even cooking) and put it in the oven on a baking tray (sheet). Roast for 12–14 minutes, depending on the size of the meat. Leave to rest for 5–10 minutes on a board.

Place the hay in the bottom of a large casserole dish with a close-fitting lid and carefully ignite (in a well-ventilated place) with a match. When it starts to burn, lay the rack on top of the hay, plonk the lid on top and leave for 5 minutes. This is sufficient time for the smoke to infuse the meat. To serve, remove the meat from the hay. Carve between the rib bones for pink, juicy, yet slightly smoky venison chops.

VENISON MULLIGATAWNY

Serves 10 *All year round*

Mulligatawny hails straight from the days of the Empire. Originally, this recipe came from Sri Lanka (or Ceylon, as it would have been known in the days of the Raj). Mulligatawny roughly translates to 'firewater', which gives you an idea of what the finished soup ought to be like! It shouldn't be the super-thick, brown meaty concoction out of cans we grew up with, but instead a thin, aromatic and spicy soup, with small shards of tender meat and grains of just-cooked rice – you could call it a 'drinking curry'. Mulligatawny is perfect with venison, but feel free to use beef or lamb, and make it as hot (or not) as you like.

75ml/2½fl oz/¼ cup vegetable
    or corn oil
6 cloves of garlic, peeled and
    finely chopped
5 large onions, peeled and very
    finely diced
500g/1lb 2oz venison, beef or
    lamb mince
2 tbsp garam masala
1 tbsp ground cumin
2 tsp turmeric
1 tsp ground ginger

2 cinnamon sticks
6 curry leaves
2 bay leaves
2 (or more – it's up to you) hot green
    or red chillies (chiles), finely chopped
4 tbsp tomato ketchup or tomato
    purée (paste)
2 litres/3½ pints/8½ cups
    chicken or lamb stock
2 handfuls of basmati rice
sea salt and freshly ground black pepper

Heat the oil in a large, heavy, flameproof casserole on the hob. Add the garlic and onions and sweat over a medium heat for 10 minutes. Remove the softened onions and garlic from the pan and put to one side.

Add the mince to the pan and cook for 10 minutes, until well browned. Add the onions back in with all the spices, the curry and bay leaves and the chillies. Stir well and cook for 5 minutes over a medium heat. Add the tomato ketchup and pour in the stock. Bring to the boil, then simmer gently for 1 hour, covered, and taste for seasoning – you will need quite a lot of seasoning to get the most out of this soup.

Add the rice and cook for a further 15 minutes. Remove the chillies and cinnamon stick. Serve hot with glasses of cold lager.

POTTED MEAT

Makes 10 small ramekins   *All year round*

The technique of potting meat has changed little through the centuries. It was hugely useful to people who had no refrigeration because it meant that meat could be kept safely for months in a larder. From my point of view it is an incredibly easy way of using up scraps of meat that would otherwise have to be minced, and turning them into a delicious dish that has the advantage of keeping for ages.

This recipe can be applied to any dark meat, and with some adaptation to any meat at all. I am using venison because the results seem to be especially good, but beef, lamb and, to a degree, pork, all work well. Essentially we are cooking the meat slowly, with plenty of added flavour in the form of spices, pounding it, then while it is still sterile and hot, sealing it into pots with a layer of fat.

200g/7oz smoked streaky bacon, rinds
   removed but reserved, chopped
1 star anise
1 cinnamon stick
1 clove
5 juniper berries
2 bay leaves
1 shoulder of venison, boned and
   roughly chopped

250g/9oz/1¼ cups unsalted
   butter, plus the same again for sealing
1 litre/1¾ pints/4¼ cups red wine
1 whole bulb of garlic, cut in half
5 sprigs of thyme
12 sage leaves
sea salt and freshly ground black pepper

Preheat the oven to 130°C/260°F/gas mark ¾. Place the bacon rinds, spices and bay leaves into a large piece of muslin (cheesecloth) and tie it into a bag with string. Place in the bottom of a casserole, then add the bacon, venison, butter, wine, garlic, thyme and 2 sage leaves and season with salt and pepper. Stir. Cover with greaseproof paper and a tight-fitting lid and cook in the oven overnight, or for approximately 8 hours.

Fish out and discard the muslin bag and its contents and remove the half-bulbs of garlic, then spoon the venison and bacon into a food processor and blitz until coarse, adding the cooking liquor in a steady stream. You are looking for the consistency of a coarse, moist paste. The fat from the melted butter will keep the potted meat moist.

Prepare 10 clean small ramekins (or jars) by putting them in an oven at 100°C/200°F/gas mark ⅛ for 1 hour. Fill the pots three-quarters full with hot meat paste, then cover with warm melted butter or goose fat. (This layer needs to be at least 5mm/¼ inch thick). Drop a sage leaf into each ramekin. Leave until the butter is firm. Keep in the fridge or larder until needed; these should keep for at least 1 month. Serve with homemade apple and pear chutney (see page 228).

HARE RAGU WITH PAPPARDELLE

Serves 10 *September to February*

This is one of the few non-British recipes in this book, but it is one of the best ways to serve hare; the dish is not so insanely strongly flavoured that the average person can't eat it.

The recipe makes use of an item of cooking equipment that you will probably find in your attic – a pressure cooker. This piece of kit does a marvellous job of turning these ingredients into a rich, unctuous meat sauce in half the time it would take if cooked conventionally in a standard casserole dish.

1 medium-sized hare (not too old),
    gutted (see below) and jointed
100ml/3½fl oz/scant ½ cup
    extra-virgin olive oil, plus extra for
    the pasta
1 large onion, peeled and finely chopped
cloves from 1 bulb of garlic, peeled and
    finely chopped

500g/1lb 2oz cherry tomatoes
1 tsp tomato purée (paste)
1 tbsp redcurrant jelly
1 sprig of rosemary
1 x 750ml bottle of red wine
200g/7oz fresh pappardelle
100g/3½oz Parmesan
sea salt and freshly ground black pepper

Firstly, and most importantly, the hare must be fresh and ideally will have been gutted as soon as it was shot. Traditionally in this country hares are hung with their guts in, which makes for a strong meat. I insist on hares being gutted straight away, like rabbits, which produces a much milder flavour.

Start by heating half of the oil in a heavy pan, then brown the pieces of hare all over on a medium-high heat. Set aside.

Pour the rest of the oil into the pressure cooker and brown the onion and garlic over a medium heat. Add the browned hare, tomatoes, tomato purée, redcurrant jelly and rosemary, then pour in enough red wine just to cover the meat. Put the lid on the pressure cooker and cook on a low heat for 2½ hours. At the end of this time, vent the steam and pull out the pieces of hare and the rosemary.

Using a potato masher, squidge the contents of the pressure cooker to create a thick ragù sauce. Season to taste. Carefully pull the meat off the bones of the hare and add it back into the ragù.

Cook the pappardelle in a pan of boiling salted water according to the packet instructions, until perfectly *al dente*, then drain and dress the pasta with olive oil, salt and pepper. Pour the rich ragù over the pasta and liberally grate Parmesan over the top.

RABBIT AND PRUNE FAGGOTS WITH CIDER-ONION GRAVY

Serves 4   *Farmed all year round; wild Winter*

Too often when people think of rabbit, their perception is that it can be casseroled or made into a pie, and that is pretty much it. Of course, rabbit is actually a lean, healthy meat that can be used in myriad ways. This recipe is deceptively easy to prepare and makes good use of this cheap and plentiful ingredient.

One very important point when making this dish is to ensure that as much silvery sinew as possible is removed from the rabbit meat. This sinew is tenacious; it will wind itself around the blades of your food processor and make it a pain to clean.

The faggot mixture really is worth making in large quantities, then portioning and freezing – it freezes well, which means you can double or even treble the quantities, and reduce your workload for the future.

100g/3½oz stoned (pitted) prunes
4 tbsp Armagnac or cider brandy
200g/7oz boneless rabbit meat,
 sinew removed
1 chicken breast
100g/3½oz lardons, finely diced
1 tbsp wholegrain mustard
1 small bunch of oregano, chopped
a handful of dried breadcrumbs
2 tbsp vegetable oil
sea salt and freshly ground black pepper

For the cider-onion gravy
50g/2oz/¼ cup butter
2 large onions, peeled and finely sliced
500ml/17fl oz/2 generous cups cider
500ml/17fl oz/2 generous cups dark
 beef stock
1 bay leaf

Soak the prunes in the Armagnac for at least half an hour. Using your food processor, coarsely blitz the rabbit and transfer it to a bowl. Coarsely blitz the chicken and put this in the bowl too. (Don't blitz the meat too finely, as you want some texture in it.) Add the lardons to the bowl, then the mustard and oregano.

Drain the prunes. Chop them into fine dice and add them to the bowl. Lastly, add the breadcrumbs and seasoning and mix well by hand. Cover and leave the mixture to infuse in the fridge for a couple of hours.

To make the gravy, melt the butter in a large, shallow sauté pan, then add the onions. Cook over a medium heat for 30 minutes, until they are soft and golden. Pour in the cider and beef stock, bring to the boil and reduce by three-quarters. Add the bay leaf and season, then pour the gravy into an ovenproof dish, cover and set aside.

continues overleaf >

Preheat the oven to 200°C/400°F/gas mark 6. Form the rabbit mixture into patties about 5cm/2 inches in diameter. Heat the oil in another pan and brown the patties on each side until they are golden. Nestle the patties into the gravy, cover, and place in the oven for 15 minutes. Remove and serve with super-creamy mashed potato.

RABBIT PIE WITH SUET CRUST

Serves 6   *Farmed all year round; wild Winter*

When cooked slowly in large quantities of goose or duck fat (in confit), rabbit defies its critics – those who perceive it to be dry and tough – and is instead shown off to its best advantage. Rabbit cooked like this is the most beautiful, fat-free, juicy and delicious meat I know.

Rabbit pie is an iconic British dish that traditionally would have contained pieces of rabbit on the bone. Our method guarantees a hassle-free dinner in which rabbit has similarities to chicken.

The technique of cooking a rabbit in confit captures the juiciness of the meat and removes any rabbity tang that may remain from the skin of the animal. Once the rabbit has cooled, it can be pulled off the carcass in glorious flaky chunks and kept in freezer bags in the fridge, retaining its moisture for a couple of days.

2 rabbits, jointed
1.5kg/3lb 5oz goose or duck fat
 (or enough to fully cover the meat
 in the pan)
3 leeks, sliced
2 onions, peeled and finely chopped
1 bulb of fennel, finely diced
3 cloves of garlic, peeled and
 finely chopped
a little butter
a handful of sage leaves, finely chopped
1 small bunch of flat-leaf parsley,
 finely chopped

For the white sauce
250g/9oz/1¼ cups butter
200g/7oz/1⅓ cups plain
 (all-purpose) flour
1.5 litres/2½ pints/5⅔ cups milk
1 bay leaf
1 tbsp wholegrain mustard
sea salt and freshly ground black pepper

For the pastry
300g/11oz/1½ cups suet
500g/1lb 2oz/3⅓ cups plain
 (all-purpose) flour, plus extra to dust
a pinch of salt
500ml/17fl oz/2 generous cups water
milk, to glaze

continues overleaf >

Start by making the pastry. Mix the suet, flour and salt together in a bowl, then add the water and mix until you have a firm pastry. Roll in clingfilm (plastic wrap) and rest in the fridge.

Immerse the rabbit pieces in the goose or duck fat in a pan. (This is a technique called confit; it will ensure the rabbit stays juicy, but will not make it fatty.) Cook them on a low heat for 3 hours, then remove from the fat and cool. Pick the meat off the bones.

To make the white sauce, melt the butter in a pan, then add the flour. Stir over a low heat for 2 minutes, then gradually pour in the milk, stirring to avoid lumps. When the sauce is smooth and all the milk is in, add the bay leaf and cook, stirring, over a low heat for 10–15 minutes, until the sauce thickens. Once thick, add the mustard and season to taste.

Preheat the oven to 190°C/375°F/gas mark 5. Gently fry the leeks, onions, fennel and garlic in a little butter over a medium heat for 10 minutes. Add the flaked rabbit and herbs. Pour in the white sauce (as much as you need) and mix well. Transfer to a large pie dish.

Roll out the pastry on a lightly floured surface to 5mm/¼ inch thick and cover the pie. Press your thumb into the edges to create a scalloped rim. Decorate with shapes cut from the remaining pastry, if desired. Brush the pastry with milk and bake the pie for 45 minutes, or until golden.

BIRDS

BIRDS

The species of game bird that we eat the most is the pheasant. This magnificent bird, of Asian origin, can be found plucked and dressed in almost every butcher's shop between October and early February. It represents excellent value for money (they should not cost you more than £3.50 per bird in rural areas; in town they will cost a little more). I am glad to say that most supermarkets are now stocking seasonal game, which means there is no excuse for not trying it.

The bird I would most urge you to try is the wood pigeon. We have to shoot this most underrated of bird in their millions to prevent crop damage and overpopulation. I was lucky enough to spend a fantastic day in April shooting wood pigeons with one of the country's top pigeon guides, Mark Gill, in the beautiful Lincolnshire Wolds for *Countrywise*. This part of the country is largely arable and is a haven for huge numbers of wood pigeons, which, if not controlled, would cause untold financial damage to the region's farmers. The wood pigeon is excellent for outdoor cooking. You can buy them on the internet – buy breasts to start with and follow the recipes in this chapter (see pages 84–6).

Quail is a popular sporting game bird in Europe and prized for its qualities as food. Not shot as a game bird in Britain, the quail is, however, farmed much like chickens and is thus readily available from supermarkets. These birds are small, mild in flavour and delicious, and do not require much cooking.

The Aylesbury is England's most famous duck. The problem is that the breed has almost died out. The true Aylesbury is a handsome, deep-bodied duck with a bill that is the colour of a lady's fingernail (unpainted) – that is, it should be shiny and a translucent off-white colour. Almost all ducks sold as Aylesburys are actually hybrids that have arisen after imported species such as Barbary and Peking ducks have had their wicked way.

The only breeder of pedigree Aylesbury ducks I know of in the UK is a hero called Richard Waller. His grandfather had the foresight to buy up all the remaining bloodlines of ducks 50 years ago, which has allowed Richard to keep the flock going. He breeds and kills a mere 10,000 ducks per year, and all are fully free range and looked after with real care and compassion.

He even kills them all on the farm, to prevent stress to the birds. Richard then processes the birds on site and sells them to various lucky restaurants and members of the public.

Geese have always been hugely important to Britain. Without the goose and its feathers we could not have won The Hundred Years' War; all longbow arrows were fledged with feathers from the wing of a goose, which gave the heavy armour-piercing arrowheads their stability. When you think about the hundreds and thousands of arrows needed to supply an army, you can imagine why goose was a popular dish. As well as the rich and delicious meat, the goose was important for its fat, which could be used to preserve food, or as a medicine.

The English partridge does not lend itself to rearing in large numbers for shooting; it is a wild bird that requires careful management to thrive. Thanks to conservation measures imposed by shoots in suitable areas of the country, it is growing in number and seems to have a certain future. It's a great example of how shooting and conservation go hand-in-hand. However, for the recipe on page 78 I have used a French partridge – completely different to our native partridge, but with its mild flavour it is an ideal beginner's game bird.

The best pieces of advice I can give you for all game birds are not to overcook them and not to buy them too well hung – stinky meat is unpopular and I do not believe that it improves the taste of the meat. Three or four days in a fridge is quite long enough for any bird.

POT-ROASTED QUAILS WITH MEAD, GRAPES AND RAISINS

Serves 4 *All year round*

This recipe is quite medieval in style and would have been cooked then using partridges or songbirds. However, for today's purposes, four plump little quails will work very well.

Pot-roasting is an ideal way to cook quail because it ensures moistness, and in this recipe the flavours of the mead, thyme and quail come together. Mead is one of the most ancient forms of alcohol known in these islands; a brew made from honey, it is fabulous to cook with and available in some supermarkets and on the internet.

4 oven-ready quails
1 tsp Dijon mustard
50g/2oz/¼ cup butter
200g/7oz baby onions (pearl onions),
    peeled (you can buy these frozen and
    ready peeled, aka pickling onions)
250ml/9fl oz/1¼ cups mead

1 tbsp runny honey
150ml/5fl oz/scant ⅔ cup cider
200g/7oz sweet seedless grapes
100g/3½oz/⅔ cup raisins
1 bunch of thyme
sea salt and freshly ground black pepper

Preheat the oven to 200°C/400°F/gas mark 6. Rub the quails with the mustard and season them with salt and pepper. Melt the butter in a heavy flameproof casserole over a medium-high heat (you'll need one with a lid). When it foams, add the quails and brown them on all sides. Remove them from the pan and set aside. Add the onions and brown for 10 minutes.

Deglaze the pan with the mead. Add the honey and cider and cook vigorously for 5 minutes with the lid off. Add the grapes and raisins and nestle the quails into the mixture. Tuck the sprigs of thyme between the quails, pop a lid on the pan and bake in the oven for 30 minutes.

Remove the pan from the oven, lift out the quails and check they are cooked by gently squeezing the breasts; if they're firm to the touch, they're done; if not, return them to the oven for a little longer. Now check the cooking liquor; if it looks too runny, reduce it a little more over a medium heat. Check the seasoning and add salt and pepper if necessary. Serve.

PHEASANT STROGANOFF

Serves 4 *October to 1 February*

Pheasant is a much-maligned meat. The popular view of this fabulous game bird is that it is dry, stringy and strongly flavoured. However, when it is correctly prepared and cooked, nothing could be further from the truth. This recipe is an easy way of ensuring that it is none of the above.

I cooked this dish for a bunch of guys running a small pheasant shoot near Barnard Castle in Northumberland last Winter. We were invited to film *Countrywise* and take part in one of their end-of-season days. The landscape, camaraderie and respect for the quarry were everything that I had hoped they would be.

The key to success with this recipe is to part-cook the pheasant meat and then add it back into the dish right at the end. This ensures moist, juicy pheasant.

4 pheasant breasts, skinned and sliced
150g/5oz/¾ cup butter or oil (depends
   how healthy you are feeling – butter
   is better!)
1 banana shallot, peeled and finely
   chopped
2 cloves of garlic, peeled and grated
100ml/3½fl oz/scant ½ cup dry
   white wine
200ml/7fl oz/scant 1 cup double
   (heavy) cream

4 anchovies, finely chopped
1 tsp grain mustard
2 tsp paprika
½ tsp cayenne pepper
4 cornichons (baby gherkins),
   finely chopped
1 tbsp capers, finely chopped
a handful of flat-leaf parsley,
   finely chopped
juice of 1 lemon
sea salt and freshly ground black pepper

Fry the pheasant in foaming butter in a heavy frying pan over a medium heat until it has a good golden colour – this will be enough to cook it most of the way through. Remove to a plate and set aside. Turn down the heat.

Gently sauté the shallot and garlic in the same pan until soft, then add the wine, cream, anchovies, mustard, paprika and cayenne. Turn up the heat until they are simmering, then cook for about 5 minutes until the sauce looks thick and rich. Add the cornichons and capers, return the pheasant to the pan, add the parsley and lemon juice, and cook for a few minutes, until the pheasant is cooked through. Season to taste and serve with steamed rice, if desired.

PHEASANT KIEV

Serves 4   *October to 1 February*

I have always loved the dishes of the 1970s that are now so out of fashion in the culinary world, and none more than the much-maligned and often appallingly made chicken Kiev. At a 70s' dinner party the serving of a crisp and magnificent Kiev, oozing with pungent garlic butter, would have been greeted with gasps of appreciation.

Sadly, this wonderful dish is now almost exclusively to be found in the frozen-food department of various supermarkets. So, why make it with pheasant? The pheasant is our most prolific game bird and, when not over-hung, has a firm, fibrous texture and tastes like a proper free-range chicken ought to taste. Unfortunately, the pheasant suffers from a reputation for being dry and/or too strong in flavour. The key to a good flavour is not to over-hang or overcook it, and to ensure that the juice remains in the meat after cooking.

The Kiev achieves both goals perfectly. The armoured coating of breadcrumbs prevents moisture escaping during cooking, while the garlic and marjoram butter within keeps the meat gloriously juicy – it is the best thing you can do with a pheasant.

For the Kiev
4 hen pheasant breasts (preferably
    without too many shot holes in them)
2 eggs
200ml/7fl oz/scant 1 cup milk
200g/7oz/1⅓ cups plain
    (all-purpose) flour
200g/7oz/1⅓ cups white breadcrumbs,
    ideally Panko (see page 46)
2 litres/3½ pints/8½ cups vegetable oil
a bunch of watercress, to serve
tomato ketchup, to serve

For the butter
250g/9oz/1¼ cups butter, softened
1 small bunch of marjoram,
    finely chopped
1 small bunch of flat-leaf parsley,
    finely chopped
6 cloves of garlic, peeled and grated
zest of 1 unwaxed lemon
1 tsp sea salt
freshly ground black pepper, to taste

Mix all the butter ingredients together in a bowl and, using your hands, work them until everything is fully incorporated.

Wash your hands, then lay out two sheets of clingfilm (plastic wrap), one on top of the other. Spoon the butter mixture down the middle of the clingfilm and roll it up into a tight sausage. Put this into the fridge and allow it to sit for at least an hour before use; it will keep for a fortnight (you can also store this in the freezer).

Remove the skin from the pheasant breasts. Insert a small knife into the thick end of each breast and open up a 5–7.5-cm/2–3-inch pocket in the meat. Cut a 5-mm/ ¼-inch thick round of butter off your sausage, remove the clingfilm and insert the butter in the pocket. Squidge the breast flat with your hand to close the pocket. When all the breasts are filled, remove the little muscles from the underside of them and place the filled breasts in the fridge for 30 minutes, covered.

Beat the eggs and milk together in a shallow dish. Put the flour in a second shallow dish and the breadcrumbs in a third. Dust the breasts with flour, dunk them on both sides in the egg wash, then coat completely in the breadcrumbs. Return to the egg wash and crumb them a second time. This gives you complete protection from the oil.

Heat the oil in a deep pan, or in your deep-fryer, to 180°C/350°F. Deep-fry the Kievs for 6 minutes, until golden brown. Remove, drain on a rack or kitchen paper and leave to rest for 3–4 minutes. Serve with watercress and tomato ketchup.

PARTRIDGE CASSEROLE

Serves 4 *September to 1 February*

I cooked this dish while filming *Countrywise Kitchen* on a dismal
November afternoon on a hilltop overlooking The Vale of Belvoir. We
had been filming in the fur-and-feather market at Melton Mowbray, and
I couldn't resist buying a couple of brace of lovely, plump French partridges.
The director thought it would be a fabulous idea to cook the partridges on
top of the coldest, windiest hilltop for 50 miles, because it had a good view!
This warming little dish, which takes only half an hour or so to cook, is the
perfect antidote to a freezing November day.

4 French partridges, plucked and
   oven-ready
50g/2oz/¼ cup butter
100g/3½oz smoked bacon lardons
12 small shallots, peeled
6 cloves of garlic, peeled
100g/3½oz mushrooms, ideally
   chanterelles or ceps, torn into
   large pieces

100ml/3½fl oz/scant ½ cup beef stock
   (one of the new style of jellied beef
   stock [bouillon] cubes will do fine)
1 x 75cl bottle of Pinot Noir
1 small bunch of fresh thyme
sea salt and freshly ground black pepper
crusty brown bread, to serve

Remove the breast and legs of the partridges (or ask your butcher to do this). Lay
them on a board and season well. Put the butter in a heavy casserole and put this over
a medium heat until it foams. Add the partridge pieces and cook for 5 minutes on
each side, until they are golden brown. Remove from the pan and set aside. Add the
bacon, shallots and garlic. Once these are coloured, remove them from the pan and
set aside.

Add a little more butter if necessary and throw in the mushrooms, then cook for
3–4 minutes, so they are cooked but still firm. Return the rest of the ingredients to
the casserole, then pour in the stock and enough wine to cover. Add the thyme and
simmer uncovered over a low heat for 30 minutes, until the meat is cooked, allowing
the liquid to reduce a little. Check the seasoning and serve in bowls with chunks of
crusty brown bread.

OLD-SCHOOL ROAST WOODCOCK

Serves 2 *October to 31 January*

The Eurasian woodcock, *Scolopax rusticola*, is the most highly prized game bird to be found in the UK. The woodcock migrates from Scandinavia and Siberia, reaching our shores with the arrival of cold weather, usually November onwards. Woodcock will make the same migration year after year, often returning to the same small patch of woodland. Considered difficult to shoot because of their fast jinking flight, these birds are commonly seen when one walks through an English wood in the deep wintertime. Woodcock are not only prized for their sporting nature, but are also considered to be the finest game bird of the lot to eat, certainly in my opinion. When plucked, the bird is plump, with sweet meat that is pale in colour.

Unusually for a game bird, they are cooked with their guts in; this may seem archaic, but there is good reason for it. The woodcock, and its cousin the snipe, both evacuate the contents of their guts upon taking flight, thus making the internal contents of the bird edible. The recipe that we are going to do is the old-fashioned and hard-core method. I don't necessarily expect you to follow this, but it is how woodcock really should be cooked.

2 woodcock, head and neck plucked
    and intact (this is important
    because the brains are a delicacy)
1 bunch of thyme
2 thick squares of white bread
100g/3½oz/scant ½ cup butter
4 slices of streaky bacon
4 chicken livers
1 tbsp Cognac or whisky
50ml/2fl oz/scant ¼ cup double
    (heavy) cream
sea salt and freshly ground black pepper

Preheat the oven to 200°C/400°F/gas mark 6. Bend the head of the woodcock around to its side and spear the beak through the body just in front of the thighs. Lay a couple of sprigs of thyme on each piece of bread and sit the woodcock on the bread in a roasting tin (pan). Rub butter over the breasts of the birds and season with salt and pepper. Cover with the bacon slices and roast for 18 minutes.

Once the woodcock are cooked, remove from the oven. Take them off the toast, remove the strips of bacon and allow the birds to rest on a wooden board. Using a spoon, remove the birds' guts and chop them finely with a knife. Put a small frying pan on the heat and drop in a large knob of butter. Add the chopped guts and the chicken livers and season with salt and pepper. Cook for 2 minutes, then pour in the Cognac or whisky and flame. Add the cream, warm through for another minute, then blitz with a hand blender into a pâté. Spread the pâté on the toast the woodcock was cooked on.

Remove the thighs and breasts from the bird and cut off its head. Carefully split the skull lengthways down the centre of the beak and lay the two halves of beak crossed over each other, thus presenting the cooked brains to the intrepid gastronaut! Arrange the breasts and thighs with the head at the top on a plate. Finally, garnish with the crispy bacon and serve with the pâté on toast to gasps of terrified delight.

Remember to present your guest with a teaspoon (you can guess what for!).

ROAST GOOSE WITH PORK, PRUNE AND CIDER BRANDY STUFFING

Serves 6 *September to 31 January*

The goose is our traditional Christmas bird. The turkey is an American interloper that arrived on these shores fairly recently, whereas we have been eating geese at Christmas for at least 1,000 years.

A goose is nowhere near as generous in its meat as a turkey, but in my book it is superior in every way. One goose will feed six people comfortably, which makes it expensive but worth it.

For the goose
1 x 5kg/11lb goose
1 tbsp sea salt
1 lemon, halved
1 large bunch of rosemary

For the stuffing
200g/7oz/generous 1 cup stoned
    (pitted) prunes

100ml/3½fl oz/scant ½ cup Somerset
    cider brandy
2 red onions, peeled and finely chopped
a large handful of thyme, finely chopped
500g/1lb 2oz ground pork sausagemeat
1 tbsp wholegrain mustard
100g/3½oz/scant 1 cup breadcrumbs,
    ideally Panko (see page 46)
sea salt and freshly ground black pepper

Soak the prunes for the stuffing in the cider brandy for at least 2 hours or overnight. Preheat the oven to 160°C/325°F/gas mark 3. Rub the goose skin with the sea salt, push the lemon halves and the rosemary into the body cavity and then pop the bird into a roasting tin (pan). Roast in the oven for 2 hours, draining off the fat from time to time.

Meanwhile, get on with the stuffing. Put the onions and thyme into a mixing bowl, then add the sausagemeat, mustard, breadcrumbs, salt and pepper. Remove the prunes from the cider brandy, chop them finely and add them to the sausagemeat mixture. Mix well by hand, then form into golfball-sized balls and place on a non-stick baking tray (sheet).

Remove the goose from the oven, baste it with goose fat, brush a little goose fat over the stuffing balls, and place the goose and the stuffing balls in the oven. Increase the temperature to 200°C/400°F/gas mark 6 and cook for a further 30 minutes, until cooked. Remove both from the oven. Allow the goose to rest for 15 minutes. Use a temperature probe to check the meat of the main part of the bird and the thighs has reached 70°C/160°F.

Carve the goose and serve with sprouts and bacon, red cabbage, roasted potatoes and Cumberland sauce.

WOOD PIGEON, BACON AND BLACK PUDDING SALAD

Serves 4   *All year round*

This lovely and simple way of serving wood pigeon has become a favourite at my pub and cookery school, The Pot Kiln. We are allowed to shoot pigeons throughout the year, due to a general licence granted by the government to prevent millions of pounds worth of agricultural damage, and thank goodness, for they are cheap, healthy and amazingly good eating! The key is not to over- or under-cook them.

4 pigeon breasts
200g/7oz really good smoked
    streaky bacon
200g/7oz firm black pudding
    (blood sausage)
1 tbsp vegetable oil
2 tbsp good sherry vinegar
4 large handfuls of picked, washed
    peppery salad leaves – rocket, mizuna
    and watercress are ideal
sea salt and freshly ground black pepper

For the dressings – yes, there are two!
200ml/7fl oz/1 cup balsamic vinegar
150ml/5fl oz/scant ⅔ cup olive oil
    (not fiercely strong extra-virgin)
1 tbsp wholegrain mustard
juice of 1 lemon
2 tbsp white wine vinegar
1 tbsp honey
sea salt and freshly ground black pepper

Make the dressings. Pour the balsamic into a pan and reduce it, uncovered over a medium heat, by 80 per cent, then leave to cool. When cooled it should be thick and syrupy. If it has gone too far, add a little water; if not enough, reduce some more. Pour into a small squeeze bottle.

Put the oil, mustard, lemon juice, white wine vinegar and honey into a mixing bowl and season with salt and pepper. Whisk vigorously for 30 seconds. The dressing should be thick and rich and hopefully spot-on in terms of seasoning and acidity. Pour into a small squeeze bottle and put both bottles in the fridge. The balsamic dressing will keep for several months and the mustard dressing for a couple of weeks.

Remove the skin and the little fillet muscle from the pigeon breasts and discard. This will prevent them from cooking unevenly. Lay out the pigeon breasts, season them well with salt and pepper and leave them, covered, for 10 minutes to come up to room temperature.

Preheat the grill to hot and place a sheet of baking parchment on a baking tray (sheet). Cut the bacon into lardons and the black pudding into 1cm/½-inch cubes. Place them both on the baking parchment and put under the grill, turning after a couple of minutes. We want the black pudding crisp but juicy on the inside and the bacon slightly crunchy.

Get a heavy pan searing hot, add the vegetable oil and cook the pigeon breasts for 1½ minutes on each side. Add the sherry vinegar to deglaze and let it boil away until it has all stuck to the meat in a lovely piquant glaze.

Remove the pigeon from the pan and let it rest for 4 minutes. Dress the salad leaves with some of the oil and white wine vinaigrette, then make a pile in the centre of each plate. Go round the salad with each dressing, then sprinkle the bacon and black pudding around. Finally, cut the pigeon lengthways into six slices and lay artfully over the salad. A little more balsamic over the meat and you are done. This is great served with a not-too-dry cider.

WOOD PIGEON AND PEAS WITH CIDER

Serves 8 as a starter or 4 as a main   *All year round   Outdoor*

The key to this dish is sweet petit pois and perfectly even, pink pigeon breasts. It makes a delicious starter with one breast each, or a light main course with two each. As a main course it can be served with crushed roasted new potatoes.

I have a suspicion that game goes with the food that it likes to eat. The absolute favourite food of the wood pigeon is the pea, and pigeon and peas go together like fish and chips. The damage a few thousand wood pigeons can do to a crop of young peas is remarkable, which is why it is so necessary to manage the numbers of these voracious crop raiders.

8 wood pigeon breasts
2 shallots, peeled and finely sliced
1 knob (pat) of butter
4 cloves of garlic, peeled and crushed
300ml/10fl oz/1¼ cups cider
    (preferably traditional)
1 sprig of rosemary
8 rashers of smoked streaky bacon,
    cut into lardons

olive oil
200g/7oz frozen petits pois
6 sage leaves, finely sliced
200ml/7fl oz/scant 1 cup double
    (heavy) cream
2 tsp grain mustard
sea salt and freshly ground black pepper

Remove the skin and the little fillet muscle from the pigeon breasts and discard (the little muscle has a sinew that runs through it, which, if left on, will cause the breast to shrink when cooking).

In a frying pan, gently sauté the shallots in the butter over a medium heat until soft but not coloured. Add the garlic and cook, stirring, for a further minute, then pour in the cider and add the rosemary. Boil for a few minutes to remove the alcohol.

Meanwhile, in a second frying pan, cook the lardons in their own fat until crispy. Remove them from the pan, drain on kitchen paper and set aside. Rub the pigeon breasts with olive oil, salt and pepper. Return the bacon frying pan to the heat and, when it is searing hot, add the breasts and sear them for 1½ minutes on each side, or until done. Set them aside to rest for at least 5 minutes.

While the pigeon is resting, remove the rosemary from the shallots and add the peas and sage. Stir in the cream, bacon and mustard and season (remembering that the bacon is salty).

Serve a spoonful of peas on a plate, then slice your beautifully pink pigeon breasts over the top.

SPICED SPATCHCOCKED CHICKEN WITH AIOLI

Serves 4   *All year round*

This recipe is designed for a barbecue, although you can, of course, cook it in the oven whenever you wish to. I do love a really good chicken and, truth be told, I think nearly everybody does. There is something about a chicken that has been chargrilled perfectly, especially when mixed with a healthy amount of piquant spices, that gets the juices flowing.

Spatchcocking (butterflying) is merely the technique of removing the backbone, splitting open and flattening the bird (you could apply this technique to any bird, such as a partridge or a pheasant, changing the time accordingly) – a process that dramatically speeds up the cooking time, and the cooked bird looks great.

Because this chicken is spiced, it is brilliant served with aioli, the classic French sauce that is effectively a rich and garlicky mayonnaise. The aioli is best made the day before to allow the flavours to infuse.

1 x 1.4kg/3lb chicken
1 tbsp paprika
½ tsp cayenne
1 tsp ground cumin
1 tsp ground ginger
3 tbsp vegetable oil
juice of 1 lemon
sea salt and freshly ground black pepper

For the aioli (makes a 400ml jar)
1 medium egg yolk
juice and zest of 1 unwaxed lemon
1 tsp Dijon mustard
300ml/10fl oz/1¼ cups vegetable oil
2 large cloves of garlic, peeled

Start with the aioli: whisk the egg yolk with the lemon juice and mustard. Then, whisking continuously, add a thin stream of oil (if you don't wish to exercise your arm muscles use an electric whisk). Continue adding oil until the mayonnaise is thick. Now pound the cloves of garlic in a pestle and mortar, until you have a fine paste. Whisk the garlic into the mayo, season well and leave overnight until it is positively reeking! It will keep well in a sterilized jar (see page 60) in the fridge for up to a week.

Next, prepare your chicken. Using a pair of game shears, remove the backbone from the bird. Turn the chicken over and flatten it with the heel of your hand. Remove the wishbone. With a small sharp knife, cut the thigh bone out of each leg (this will ensure even cooking). Mix all the dry ingredients together with the oil and lemon juice in a bowl, then rub the mixture into every crevice of the chicken, cover and leave to marinate in the fridge for 1 hour.

continues overleaf >

Preheat your barbecue to a low-medium heat. Impale the chicken with two diagonal skewers; this keeps it flat and even during cooking. Cook the chicken, skin side down, for 10 minutes. Turn the chicken over and repeat. Keep turning the chicken until it is cooked through, which should take about 40 minutes. If it starts to blacken, the barbecue is too hot. Check the chicken is fully cooked by piercing the thickest part of the thigh with a skewer; any sign of pink and it needs longer. (If you are cooking in the oven, roast the spatchcocked chicken for 40 minutes, or until cooked through, at 200°C/400°F/gas mark 6.) Cut it into quarters and serve with the aioli, some bread and salad.

ROAST AYLESBURY DUCK

Serves 2–4 (depends how generous you are)

The Aylesbury's qualities are legendary, and in my book the duck should be cooked fully, not pink, so that the meat is coming away from the bone when cooked. And finally, cook it simply.

1 onion, peeled
1 x 3kg/6½lb Aylesbury duck
3 bay leaves
1 tbsp sea salt
2 tbsp dark soy sauce (optional)

One of the best things about roasting a duck is the thick layer of fat that encases the whole bird. This slowly melts away when cooking, keeping the bird super-juicy.

Preheat the oven to 220°C/425°F/gas mark 7. Push the onion into the duck's cavity, follow it with the bay leaves and pop the bird on a trivet in a roasting pan. Rub the duck with salt and roast for 1½ hours. Open the oven door and brush the duck with soy sauce, if you like, then roast for a further 15 minutes. Remove the duck from the tin and rest on a wooden board for 20 minutes.

Carve into breast and thigh portions and serve piled high on a board with roasted potatoes and bread sauce. A raw cabbage coleslaw is great as well – it will cut the fattiness of the meat.

WILD TEAL CHINESE-STYLE PANCAKES

Serves 2 *October to January / Outdoor*

One of the oldest and most challenging forms of shooting in the British Isles is of wild teal. This is surely among the most rewarding forms of shooting, and I have been lucky enough to take part in a shoot on the north Norfolk coast for *Countrywise Kitchen*. The Heacham Wildfowlers' Club has been looking after a large part of the north Norfolk coast for several decades. Its members have steadily improved the habitat and done wonders for the conservation in the area. In return for all their hard work, every year each member is allowed to shoot a few geese and ducks.

Darren, who took me out, is a master of the sport and taught me a lot in the short time we spent together. It is astonishing how difficult it is, especially hitting the teal that come in early morning and late evening. They fly spectacularly quickly and plunge down to feed from a height, like a swooping peregrine. We were lucky enough to shoot three the morning we spent crouching in the reeds, and since the weather was brisk, they had cooled down by the time the sun was fully risen and we decided it was time to eat.

This dish is particularly suited to a barbecue, since it is very easy to prepare with minimal ingredients. Simply pluck the duck breasts and cut them out of the body of the bird; two per person will do admirably.

2 teal, breasts removed and plucked
2 or more large tortillas
a handful of spring onions (scallions), trimmed and cut into thin julienne
½ cucumber, cut into thin sticks
1 small bunch of coriander (cilantro), finely chopped
sea salt and freshly ground black pepper.

For the sauce
1 thumb-sized knob of fresh root ginger, peeled
50ml/2fl oz/3 tbsp maple syrup
50ml/2fl oz/3 tbsp dark soy sauce
50ml/2fl oz/3 tbsp plum sauce
50ml/2fl oz/3 tbsp hoisin sauce
juice of 2 limes

Light your barbecue. When the coals are grey hot and the flames have disappeared, make the sauce. Grate the ginger onto a piece of muslin or cheesecloth and squeeze the juice into a jam jar. Add the maple syrup, soy sauce, plum sauce, hoisin sauce and lime juice (retaining a small amount for later). Put the lid on the jar and shake vigorously. You will have a thick, syrupy and delicious dipping sauce.

Using a pastry brush, brush the duck breasts with the sauce, then grill on the hot barbecue for 2 minutes on either side, or until done. Set the duck aside and leave to rest for 2 minutes, then carve it into long pink strips and lay them down the centre of the tortillas. Add a sprinkling of spring onions, cucumber and coriander and a little dipping sauce. Fold into a wrap and enjoy while being surrounded by feathers.

SEA FISH

SEA FISH

Fish is quick to cook, easy to prepare, healthy and stunning to look at. These days, however, it is also scarce. Stocks of some species of fish are seriously depleted. As a consequence, prices have risen dramatically and for most of us what once was regarded as everyday food now has to be kept for a special occasion. Many chefs counter this by looking for less popular fish that were sniffed at 20 years ago – species such as gurnard, sardines, mackerel and the small monkfish that are inevitably caught along with their bigger cousins are now appearing on menus.

Overfishing and the wastage of by-catch is a real problem. Thankfully there are moves afoot to change this. Organisations such as the Marine Stewardship Council give out excellent advice on what we should be eating, so do have a look at their website before buying fresh fish (www.msc.org). It's great to purchase fish from small suppliers who buy off the day-boats (that is, they spend only one day at sea, thus ensuring the freshest of fish) at ports such as Newlyn and Looe. You should also try to be flexible, and buy what is freshest and offers the best value on the day.

By all means splash out on some beautiful big, thick fillets of cod, so long as they have come from a controlled, sustainable fishery. But we should consider this akin to buying aged fillets of beef. To continue the analogy, if you want to eat steak a lot, then use rump (or in our case, buy mackerel or gurnard). A good example is the Dover sole recipe on page 108; I was being extravagant in choosing this fish, I admit it, but there is no reason why you cannot substitute a lovely plaice or lemon sole.

One of the best experiences to be had is to go sea-fishing. I believe that to understand an ingredient and to be inspired by it, you need to experience it in its own environment. I go sea-fishing at least three or four days every summer, and always come back completely rabid about cooking fish. When you catch fish by rod and line, you make it personal. When you charter a boat for the day you are doing a really good thing; not only will you learn new skills from a master fisherman, but you will also get to take lots of fish home to family and friends, and support a fishing family in the process. Our fishing communities are so important to the coastal fabric of Britain, and we should support them to the hilt.

Farmed fish are playing a crucial role in supplying the British public. Almost all the sea bass and bream we eat, and even species such as turbot, are now being successfully farmed, and provide a very good product. Make sure you know the provenance of what you are buying.

Shellfish and crustaceans thrive in our waters. In fact, the decline in big cod has been a real boon to young crabs and lobsters, for cod were one of their principle enemies. I think few things in summertime appeal as much to the British public as the sweet white meat to be found in our native brown crab. For me, it is close to being an addiction. If I ever get the opportunity to purchase a large cock crab, freshly caught (that is, within a couple of days of coming out of the sea), then I do so without hesitation.

Crabs are plentiful as long as they are fished for in a sensible and sustainable manner. They represent amazing value for money when compared to a lobster. However, the native British lobster is the finest in the world, blowing the Maine lobster out of the water. Other shellfish we should eat include langoustines, most of which tragically go to Spain. Possibly the classiest of all is the fabulous scallop, which abounds around our coast. If you are thinking of indulging, I would beg that you ask the fishmonger how they were caught, since dredged scallops are ethically wrong in my book. You want to find hand-dived scallops, which have been selectively picked.

Treat all these lovely creatures with the utmost respect and please do not overcook them; it's a crime against nature.

MONKFISH TAILS ROASTED WITH CAPERS, BACON AND PARSLEY WITH MARSH SAMPHIRE

Serves 4   *August to January*

Monkfish was for many years considered a by-catch. Arguably the ugliest fish to swim in the oceans, this deep-water hunter is regularly caught in our nets and has become very fashionable. Its rich, thick chunks of white meat are almost chicken-like in texture and it makes a very hearty main course.

I love great big monkfish tails that can be cut into beautiful fillets, but these can be hard to get. In this day and age it is very important that any by-catch be consumed, so I use baby monkfish tails. These are being caught as part of the everyday catch and, if thrown back, would not survive the return journey to depth. So let us make use of them.

The beautiful thing about a 200–300g/7–11oz monkfish tail is that it is a one-portion serving. Get it skinned from the fishmonger.

100g/3½oz/scant ½ cup butter
4 x 250g/9oz monkfish tails
2 unwaxed lemons, finely grated
2 large shallots, peeled and
    finely chopped
1 clove of garlic, peeled and
    finely chopped
100g/3½oz smoked bacon lardons,
    very finely chopped

2 tbsp baby capers
75ml/⅓ cup dry white wine
1 small bunch of flat-leaf parsley,
    very finely chopped
sea salt and freshly ground black pepper
a large handful of marsh samphire,
    to serve

Preheat the oven to 200°C/400°F/gas mark 6. Heat a large, non-stick ovenproof pan over a medium-high heat. Add a decent-sized knob (pat) of butter and, when it foams, nestle the monkfish tails in and brown them on both sides. Season with salt and pepper, squeeze the juice of half a lemon over the fish and transfer to the oven to bake for 10 minutes. Check the fish is hot throughout; since monkfish tails vary in size, you will need to exercise judgement. Push a skewer or knife into the thick part of the fish – if it comes out hot, the fish will be done; it should take no more than 15 minutes. Remove the fish from the oven, take it out of the pan and allow it to rest.

Meanwhile, add the rest of the butter to the pan and throw in the shallots, garlic and lardons. Cook over a high heat for a few minutes, until the bacon is cooked. Add the

continues overleaf >

capers, squeeze in the remaining lemon juice, and add the zest of both lemons. Pour in the white wine. Toss in the pan for 2–3 minutes, then add the parsley and toss once or twice more.

Pour boiling water over the samphire, then drain and lay out on a platter. Lay the monkfish tails on the bed of samphire and then spoon the bacon and caper mix over the top.

CORNISH CHOWDER WITH ROASTED COD

Serves 4 *Winter*

The beaches and coastline of Cornwall are perfect for foraging for cockles, mussels and clams. They can be easily sourced – and if you can't find them wild you can easily buy them. Be sure to only forage from clean water though. Wash any wild shellfish well and check they are alive and healthy at the time of cooking.

There are quite a few elements to this dish, but do not be daunted by them; it is very easy!

4 x 120–150g/4–5oz pieces of cod, preferably centre fillet, nice and thick
4 bay leaves
50g/2oz/¼ cup butter
4 large shallots, peeled and finely chopped
1 clove of garlic, peeled and finely chopped
2 sticks (stalks) of celery, finely chopped
100g/3½oz smoked bacon lardons, finely diced
175ml/6fl oz/⅔ cup cider or dry white wine
200g/7oz medium-sized mussels, washed and prepared (see page 116)

200g/7oz small clams, washed and prepared (see page 116)
200g/7oz cockles (baby clams), washed and prepared (see page 116)
200ml/7fl oz/scant 1 cup fish stock
200ml/7fl oz/scant 1 cup double (heavy) cream
200g/7oz small Jersey Royal or other small new potatoes, quartered, boiled and cooled
a small handful of chervil
juice of 1 lemon
sea salt and freshly ground black pepper

Cut a small incision laterally into the centre of each piece of cod. Slide a bay leaf into each pocket so the leaf sticks out either side. Now put the cod to one side.

Melt the butter in a heavy pan over a medium heat. Add the shallots, garlic and celery. The heat should not be too high, as we want these vegetables to soften but not brown. Cook for a few minutes. Turn the heat up a little and add the bacon. Cook for 2–3 minutes more, then add the cider, then all the shellfish and turn the heat up

continues overleaf >

to high. Pour in the fish stock and cream. Add the boiled new potatoes and cook for about 5 minutes.

Meanwhile, preheat the grill to hot. Sprinkle the cod with salt and pepper and place, skin side up, under the grill for 4–5 minutes, until the fish is just firm. Remove the fish from under the grill and let it rest.

Take the seafood chowder off the heat and check the seasoning. Discard any shellfish that remain closed. Add salt and pepper if necessary. Spoon the chowder into bowls, distributing the vegetables evenly. Lay the cod on top and sprinkle with a little chopped chervil and a squeeze of lemon. Serve with crisp cold Provence rosé.

ROAST HAKE WITH SWEET-AND-SOUR PEPPERS

Serves 4   *October to March*

The hake is a magnificent predator that hunts the waters off Britain's coast.

This ugly, snaggle-toothed, 90cm/3-foot or more long, piscine killing machine has stunning milky-white flesh that is exquisitely sweet, if quite high on the bone count. The problem is that we don't see much hake in British supermarkets. This is because most of our hake are bought and devoured by the rapacious Spanish and Portuguese markets. It's a terrible shame and one that can be rectified by asking for hake at your local fishmonger; all we have to do is outbid the Spanish!

I love combining the flavour of a whole roasted hake with the sweet sharpness of peppers cooked in the Italian method known as *agrodolce*. These peppers are simple to prepare and this combination is delicious. The whole dish is finished with a simple green sauce made from basil, parsley, lemon and olive oil.

1 x 2–2.5kg/4½–5½lb hake (I like to
    serve this fish with the head on), scaled and gutted
100ml/3½fl oz/scant ½ cup olive oil
sea salt and freshly ground black pepper

For the peppers
50ml/2fl oz/scant ¼ cup extra-virgin
    olive oil
8 red (bell) peppers, deseeded and
    thinly sliced
2 cloves of garlic, peeled and sliced
100g/3½oz/½ cup soft brown sugar
100ml/3½fl oz/scant ½ cup red
    wine vinegar

For the green sauce
1 small bunch of basil, leaves picked
1 small bunch of flat-leaf parsley,
    leaves picked
juice of 2 lemons
50ml/2fl oz/scant ¼ cup extra-virgin
    olive oil

Preheat the oven to 180°C/350°F/gas mark 4.

Start with the peppers. Heat the olive oil in a large heavy pan over a medium heat. Add the peppers and garlic. Cook for 30 minutes, until soft. Add the sugar and vinegar, turn the heat down to low and cook for a further 30–40 minutes, until most of the liquid has disappeared. The peppers will taste deliciously sweet and yet a little tart from the vinegar.

Meanwhile, brush the hake with the olive oil and sprinkle it with sea salt, then put it into a roasting tin (pan). Bake for 30 minutes, or until a knife pushed into a thick part of the fish is hot when it is pulled out – then you will know that the fish is cooked right the way through.

To make the green sauce, put the basil and parsley leaves, lemon juice and olive oil in a blender and whizz until fine, then season with salt and pepper.

Spoon the peppers into a large oval serving dish. Carefully fillet the hake, then lay the fillets down the centre of the peppers. Spoon some of the green sauce over the top of the fish to finish.

I serve this with chilled Sauvignon Blanc or something similar.

FLAME-GRILLED MACKEREL WITH HARISSA

Serves 4   *June to October*

One of my absolute best *Countrywise Kitchen* experiences took place off the eerie Kentish coast, near the nuclear power station at Dungeness. I was taken out fishing for the ultimate in sustainable fish – the humble, yet awesomely delicious mackerel. This shoaling predator is voracious, living off whitebait, and when you catch them, boy, do you catch them! The skipper of our boat was called Trevor. His main job is as the engineer of the Dungeness Lifeboat. A softly spoken seaman, Trevor took us straight to the fish, about three miles offshore, where I caught 50 mackerel in about 30 minutes. Gutted on the spot, they were quickly taken to the beach for cooking.

Harissa is an amazing condiment that is endemic in North African cookery. Essentially a mashed-up mix of red chillies, garlic, olive oil and possibly coriander, it is delicious, and only as hot as the chillies you use – it's up to you. Brilliant for barbecues and with everything grilled, it is especially good on super-fresh fish like our mackerel. All you need for this dish is mackerel, harissa and some long metal skewers.

4 x 450g/1lb mackerel, gutted
   and cleaned
1 lemon, cut into wedges, to serve

For the harissa
6 medium-hot red chillies (chiles),
   deseeded and finely chopped
12 fat cloves of garlic, peeled and
   finely chopped

1 small bunch of coriander (cilantro), finely
   chopped (stalks and leaves kept separate)
1 tsp coriander seeds
1 tsp cumin seeds
1 tbsp sea salt
6 tbsp olive oil
1 lemon

Light your barbecue and wait until the flames have died down and the coals have gone grey. It needs to be hot.

Start by making the harissa. Place the chillies, garlic and coriander in a pestle and mortar with the coriander and cumin seeds. Add the salt and half the oil and grind slowly into a paste. When smoothish (take your time), add the rest of the oil and the juice of the lemon. This paste will keep for a week or so in the fridge.

Slash the mackerel three or four times on each side. Rub the harissa over the fish inside and out and skewer or place the fish in a fish grill. Grill it for 5 minutes on each side or until it is cooked through, making sure it chars a little but does not burn. Serve with wedges of lemon and chilled white wine – and a finger bowl.

SOUSED MACKEREL

Serves 12 *June to October*

I love the idea of pickling things, and pickled fish are a British institution that goes back hundreds, if not thousands, of years. Traditionally, we pickled oily fish, by which I mean sardines, herrings and mackerel, since their firm texture and oily nature stand up to the pickling process admirably. It goes without saying that you must use the freshest of fish, with the shiniest eyes and the reddest gills. If the mackerel has lost its sheen it is not fresh enough.

This recipe is magnificent for a hot Summer lunch in the garden. The fish is tart, sweet and sour all at the same time, and cries out to be eaten with homemade bread and delicious creamy butter. Very cold rosé is essential.

675ml/1 pint 2½fl oz/2¾ cups of white
    wine vinegar
225g/8oz/1 cup of caster (superfine) sugar
6 large shallots, peeled and finely sliced
3 bay leaves
2 star anise
1 tbsp celery seeds
zest of 2 unwaxed lemons
75ml/2½fl oz/5 tbsp olive oil
12 mackerel, gutted, cleaned and filleted
sea salt and freshly ground black pepper

Bring the vinegar up to a medium heat in a steel saucepan. Add the sugar and let it dissolve over the heat, then leave to cool.

Once the vinegar is cool, add the shallots, along with the bay leaves, star anise, celery seeds, lemon zest and oil. Add a good pinch of salt and several twists of black pepper. Stir and taste for seasoning, then lay out the mackerel fillets in a deep baking tray (sheet) and completely cover with the mixture. Cover and leave for 24 hours in the fridge before serving. The soused mackerel will keep very well in a clean sealed container for a week in the fridge.

SEA BASS WITH BRAISED FENNEL, CIDER AND CREAM

Serves 2 *Summer*

The sea bass is the king of British game fish. This voracious predator hunts around our shores and grows slowly up to a maximum of about 6.8kg/15lb in weight. Unlike a lot of fish in our oceans, the sea bass seems to be doing rather well.

Delicious, firm, white flesh with a meaty texture, sea bass is hugely popular in home kitchens and restaurant kitchens alike. It is awesome cooked whole on a barbecue and goes well with fennel, an underused vegetable.

The sea bass is highly sought-after by anglers for its fighting abilities and because it is one of the few fish in British waters that can be taken on a fly. A large line-caught sea bass of 1.4kg/3lb or more is a magnificent feast that it is well worth whatever you have to pay for it.

1 large bunch of rosemary
4 tbsp olive oil
1 x 1.4kg/3lb sea bass, gutted, scaled and cleaned
100g/3½oz/½ cup butter
4 small fennel bulbs, quartered

200ml/7fl oz/scant 1 cup medium cider
1 lemon
200ml/7fl oz/scant 1 cup double (heavy) cream
sea salt and freshly ground black pepper

Preheat the oven to 200°C/400°F/gas mark 6. Lay the rosemary in a roasting tin (pan). Oil the sea bass, sprinkle it liberally with salt and pepper, place it on a baking tray (sheet) and roast it in the oven for 25–30 minutes, depending on size.

Meanwhile, melt the butter in a heavy frying pan over a medium heat, then lightly brown the fennel for 10 minutes on each side. Pour in the cider, increase the heat to high, and cook to reduce the liquid by half. Add the juice of half the lemon, pour in the cream and reduce for a second time. Check the fennel is soft but still retains some bite. Remove the fish from the oven.

Allow the sea bass to rest for a few minutes, add any roasting juices from the fish to the cream-and-cider sauce, then gently pull the fillets off the fish, trying to keep them in one piece.

Spoon the fennel, cider and cream sauce into deep plates and place the fish over the top. Finish with a squeeze from the remaining half of the lemon and serve with a glass of chilled dry white wine.

DOVER SOLE WITH BROWN SHRIMP BUTTER

Serves 2 *All year round*

The brown shrimp is another iconic British ingredient. Traditionally hoovered up from places such as Morecambe Bay on the north-western coast of England, these stunningly delicious little morsels were a Victorian staple. They are hard to beat in their traditional form, which is potted in butter and then spread on toast with a squeeze of lemon, but I felt we needed something a little more involved for this book.

A handful of brown shrimps lightly warmed in brown butter lift and complement most of our British sea fish. In this instance, I am going to use a Dover sole, which is extravagant, but then so are brown shrimps. If you can't get sole, a thick slice of plaice or lemon sole should do well as a substitute. We really don't want to muck around with the fish too much. They all taste fabulous in their own right, so less is definitely more.

4 Dover soles or tranches of brill or turbot, gutted
olive oil, to grease
100g/3½oz/½ cup butter
juice of 2 lemons
200g/7oz peeled brown shrimps
a handful of parsley, finely chopped
2 tbsp baby capers
sea salt and freshly ground black pepper

Preheat the grill to medium. Place the fish on a sheet of oiled aluminium foil set on a grill tray. Dot the fish with a few small pieces of butter and sprinkle over some salt and pepper. Squeeze the juice of 1 lemon over the fish and place under the hot grill, skin side up, for 4–5 minutes, or until cooked through – make sure the fish is reasonably far from the element so as not to burn the skin; we want crispy, not black.

Place a heavy pan on the stove and leave to heat for 2 minutes. The heat should be medium-high, but not scorching. Cut the rest of the butter into small knobs (pats) and throw it in the pan – it will start to sizzle. Allow the butter to gently change colour until it is golden brown; the French call this *beurre noisette* or hazelnut butter, which is because the brown butter should smell nutty. Once it reaches this point, squeeze in the juice of the remaining lemon, add the brown shrimps, parsley and capers and warm through for a minute or so. Grind in plenty of black pepper.

Place the fish in the centre of a gleaming white plate and spoon the brown shrimp butter liberally over it. Serve with a little cooked marsh samphire.

GRILLED SARDINES WITH TOMATO SAUCE

Serves 4 *Summer*

The sardine, or pilchard as it can be known in this country, is one of the humblest, yet to my mind finest, fish to be found around our shores. I am obsessed with its staggeringly delicious flavour. Simply grilled over charcoal, brushed with a little lemon juice and olive oil during cooking, and sprinkled with sea salt, it tastes sublime.

Served with garlic-rubbed grilled bread and a chunkily made rough tomato sauce redolent of garlic and rosemary, it captures the essence of cheap and sustainable seafood.

The problem with sardines is that they must be fresh; they need to be shining silver, with gleaming eyes, and ideally stiff as a board.

50ml/2fl oz/¼ cup olive oil
juice of 2 lemons, plus extra lemon
    wedges to serve
12 fat Cornish sardines, gutted, scaled
    and cleaned
1 small bunch of rosemary
4 slices of thick ciabatta or
    focaccia-style bread
2 cloves of garlic, peeled
a handful of basil leaves, torn (optional)

For the tomato sauce
100ml/3½fl oz/scant ½ cup olive oil
4 cloves of garlic, peeled and sliced
1 red chilli (chile)
750g/1lb 11oz ripest cherry tomatoes
125ml/4fl oz/½ cup dry white wine
sea salt and freshly ground black pepper

Start with the tomato sauce. Warm the oil in a heavy pan over a medium heat, add the garlic and leave to infuse on a low heat for 10 minutes. Prick the chilli several times with the tip of a knife to allow the flavour to escape. Add the tomatoes and chilli to the oil and cook over a low heat for 40 minutes. Add the wine and a sprinkling of salt and plenty of pepper. Turn the heat up slightly, then crush to a rough sauce using a potato masher and simmer for 5 minutes more.

While the sauce is cooking, light your barbecue and wait until the flames have died down and the coals have gone grey, or preheat your grill to medium. Now for the sardines. Mix the oil and lemon juice together in a bowl. Place the sardines over the barbecue or under the grill. Brush with the oil and lemon mixture and sprinkle with salt. Cook for 4–5 minutes, then turn the fish and repeat until cooked through, brushing with the oil and lemon as you do so.

Just before you finish cooking, throw the rosemary on the coals to infuse the sardines with a final blast of flavour. Rub the bread with the garlic, brush with a little more oil and grill until crisp. Serve the sardines on plates with the tomato sauce spooned over the toast, adding lemon wedges and torn basil leaves to finish if you wish.

PEPPERY CRAB SALAD

Serves 4 *March to August*

There is most certainly a knack in the preparation of a cooked crab, but step-by-step guides are easily found on the internet. Suffice it to say, you will need a hammer, a pair of gloves and a long-bladed pick for getting the white meat out of all the nooks and crannies. We must not forget the brown meat contained in a crab – when made into a mayonnaise this is delicious on toast. So for this recipe we will serve the two meats side by side.

1 x 1.8kg/4lb cock crab
1 bunch of young peppery watercress,
   finely chopped
1 tsp sweet paprika

For the mayonnaise
1 egg yolk
1 tbsp white wine vinegar

juice of 1 lemon
1 tsp Dijon mustard
100ml/3½fl oz/scant ½ cup
   extra-virgin olive oil
1 litre/1¾ pints/4¼ cups vegetable oil
sea salt and freshly ground black pepper

I put the crab in the freezer for 1 hour prior to cooking; this seems to put it to sleep gently and hopefully reduces the shock of boiling. Boil the crab in plenty of salted water for 20 minutes. Plunge it into a sink of iced water to stop the cooking process.

Meanwhile, make the mayonnaise. Tip the egg yolk into a large mixing bowl, add the vinegar, lemon juice and mustard and whisk together (old-fashioned electric whisks work well for this). Anchor the mixing bowl on a cloth, then, whisking with one hand, start pouring in the olive oil with the other, in a very slow stream (pour too fast and it will split). Keep going until you have used all the oil and you will see the mayonnaise start to emulsify and thicken, then switch to vegetable oil to lighten the mayonnaise. Keep pouring in a thin, steady stream, whisking continuously until the mayonnaise is as thick as you would like it. Season with salt and pepper and place in the fridge.

Twist off the crab's claws and legs. Remove the top shell and discard the small stomach sac just behind the crab's mouth and the soft gills that are attached along the edges of the centre part. Pick the white meat from the claws and shell of your crab, reserving the brown meat. In a separate bowl, combine the white crab meat with the watercress and 2 large spoonfuls of mayonnaise. Fold and spoon into a bowl. Sprinkle with sweet paprika and serve with brown crab on toast (see page 114).

BROWN CRAB ON TOAST

Serves 4 *March to August*

1 tbsp mayonnaise (see page 112)
cooked brown meat from a 1.8kg/4lb cock crab (see page 112)
a few drops of Tabasco
½ tbsp brandy
sea salt and freshly ground black pepper
4 pieces of toast, to serve

Stir the mayonnaise, crab meat, Tabasco and brandy together in a bowl and season to taste. Serve on toast beside the Peppery crab salad on page 112.

NORTH DEVON SEAFOOD LUNCH

Serves 4   *January to April*

One of the lovely things about foraging for your lunch is that you cook only what you can find. This forces you to be creative and use your hard-found ingredients wisely. One of my favourite *Countrywise* experiences was on a filthy day in north Devon. My guide was a salty north Devon (by way of London) man called Dan the Fish Man. Dan fishes and sells his catch both locally and into London, but his real passion is foraging. The tide on the day in question meant that we had to be on site at 5am (no problem for me, deerstalking in June requires 3am wakeups, so 5am is a lie-in). But the crew looked a little piqued, especially as the whole coast was blanketed in fog and rain. Still, *Countrywise* is a real programme and we film in any conditions!

The quantity of perfect seafood was amazing, with winkles, limpets and tiny mussels in abundance. Best of all was the sea purslane and sea beet growing on the shore. We picked enough for lunch and went back to Appledore to cook breakfast.

Even at that time of year there were loads of people on the seafront eating lunch – so Sassy, my canine companion, could indulge in some world-class scrounging while we cooked.

250g/9oz generous 1¼ cups butter
500g/1lb 2oz winkles, washed and
    prepared (see page 116)
500g/1lb 2oz tiny mussels, washed and
    prepared (see page 116)
250g/9oz limpets, washed and
    prepared (see page 116)
1 bottle of cider

100ml/3½fl oz double (heavy) cream
a double handful of sea beet
a double handful of wild garlic
    or spinach
a handful of purslane
*(if you can't get any of these vegetables,
    use watercress instead)*
freshly ground black pepper

Melt half the butter in a heavy pan over a medium heat (ideally on a camping stove!), and add the winkles, mussels and limpets. Cook for 3 minutes, then add a glassful of cider and cook for another minute. Add a good splash of double cream and cook for 1 minute more, then season with pepper. Discard any shellfish that have failed to open.

In a separate pan, add a big lump of butter (how much is up to you) and let it foam. Add the sea beet, wild garlic or spinach and purslane, toss in the butter for 1 minute, then add a splash of cider.

Serve the greens and the seafood together in a big bowl – provide a pin for the winkles, and expect to get messy – and drink the rest of the cider!

LINGUINE WITH TOMATO, CLAMS AND CRAB

Serves 4 *Summer*

While the focus of this book is on British food and ingredients, I felt I had to include a couple of recipes for pasta. This simple combination of egg and flour in its many forms has become a national staple – everybody eats it and has a favourite recipe. This is my favourite pasta dish, and one that I never get tired of cooking and eating. The colours and flavours of this dish are definitely summery: juicy tomatoes, pungent garlic, delicate white crab meat and delicious fresh clams combined with a dash of vivid green from the flat-leaf parsley to give a bowl of pasta that delights the eye and makes a mess of your shirt! The key to this is the gentle infusion of the tomatoes and garlic in the fruity olive oil, so keep the heat down and take your time.

100ml/3½fl oz/scant ½ cup
   extra-virgin olive oil
6 cloves of garlic, peeled and finely
   chopped
500g/1lb 2oz ripe baby plum tomatoes
   or cherry tomatoes, halved
200g/7oz dried linguine
juice of ½ lemon

75ml/5 tbsp dry white wine
24 small clams, washed and prepared
   (see below)
200g/7oz cooked white crab meat
1 small bunch of flat-leaf parsley,
   roughly chopped
sea salt and freshly ground black pepper

Heat a large frying pan over a low-medium heat and add the oil to a depth of about 5mm/¼ inch. Add the garlic; it should not sizzle when it goes in the oil. Add the tomatoes and simmer for 15–20 minutes until they start to break down. Meanwhile, cook the pasta in plenty of salted boiling water for 8–10 minutes, until *al dente*. Drain.

Increase the heat under the pan of tomatoes slightly and add the lemon juice and wine. Simmer for 2 minutes, then squash the contents of the pan gently with a potato masher. Add the clams and cook for 2 minutes until they open; discard any that don't open. Take off the heat, then stir in the crab meat and parsley. Season to taste and mix with the linguine. Have plenty of fresh bread and chilled white wine available.

How to prepare mussels, clams, cockles, winkles and limpets

Put the shellfish in a washing up bowl of cold water. Scrub them using a small stiff brush to remove any barnacles, sand or grit. Pull any beard off the mussels. Discard any shellfish that are broken or that are open and do not close when tapped against the side of the sink. Once cooked, discard any shellfish that have failed to open.

COCKLES WITH CIDER AND CREAM

Serves 4 *January to April*

Cockles are possibly our most modest and unassuming shellfish. For me, however, the humble cockle is among the sweetest and most delicious morsels to be found on Britain's seashore. Cunningly hidden inches below the sand and mud, the cockle can typically be found in such beauty spots as the Gower peninsula of South Wales, where they have been a source of food for the locals for millennia.

The man who taught me to riddle for cockles on the Gower is a magnificent Welshman called Randolph Jenkins. Randolph and his family have been gathering and eating cockles for as many generations as they can remember. Sadly, the Gower beaches have been heavily harvested by commercial cocklers and the cockle population is a shadow of its former self. We collected a modest bucketful and cooked them, together with a few local mussels that had found their way into our riddles, with some local Welsh cider and some excellent double cream.

100g/3½oz/½ cup butter
1 leek, finely chopped
3 banana shallots, peeled and finely chopped
1 clove of garlic, peeled and finely chopped
100ml/3½fl oz/scant ½ cup dry cider
150ml/5fl oz/scant ⅔ cup double (heavy) cream
1kg/2¼lb fresh cockles (baby clams), washed and prepared (see page 116)
500g/1lb 2oz mussels, washed and prepared (see page 116)
a handful of flat-leaf parsley, roughly chopped
juice of 1 lemon
sea salt and freshly ground black pepper

Heat up a heavy saucepan or casserole over a medium heat and add the butter. When it foams, add the leek, shallots and garlic and cook for 5 minutes, until softened but not browned. Add the cider and cook for a further 3 minutes, then pour in the cream. Tip in the cockles and mussels, throw in the parsley, add the lemon juice, salt and pepper, turn the heat up to high and cook with the lid on for 3 minutes. Discard any shellfish that haven't opened. Serve with chunks of white bread and mugs of cider.

LOBSTER ON THE BARBECUE

Serves 4   *June to November*

I am lucky enough to have met some wonderful people while filming *Countrywise*. One of the most memorable was Joe Miller, whose family have been fishing for crabs and lobsters off Lulworth Cove in Dorset for several hundred years.

Unfortunately, when most of us think of lobster, we think of a bright-red, terrifyingly expensive crustation that often doesn't live up to its price tag in terms of flavour. This is partly because many lobsters that are available to the consumer are imported from the east coast of the USA, have been out of the water for a considerable period of time, and when they are cooked have lost condition.

Our native lobster is a magnificent blue/black creature and I am pleased to say that in this time of seafood shortages it is doing very well indeed as a species. We sailed out of Lulworth Cove, pulled up a couple of 700g/1½lb beauties, sailed back in, lit a fire on the beach, and grilled them then and there. For those of you wishing to do the same thing: fires are not permitted on Lulworth beach – TV has its privileges!

2 x 700g/1½lb lobsters
250g/9oz/1¼ cups butter
2 lemons
2 large shallots, peeled and finely chopped
4 cloves of garlic, peeled and finely chopped
1 x 750ml bottle dry white wine, chilled
1 large bunch of flat-leaf parsley, finely chopped
sea salt and freshly ground black pepper

Light your barbecue and wait until the flames have died down and the coals have gone grey and are hot, or preheat your grill to medium.

Take each lobster, and place a large, sharp knife on the 'T' behind its head. Push down hard with the point of the knife. Cut the lobsters in half lengthways using the knife, then lay them, cut-side up, on the barbecue.

Put a couple of dots of butter on each lobster half and give them a little squeeze of lemon. Cook them for 8–10 minutes or until cooked through, turning them over just before the end of the cooking time. The meat should pull away from the shell and be firm to the touch when it is cooked.

continues overleaf >

Meanwhile, cut two-thirds of the remaining butter into small dice and set aside. Add the remaining one-third of the butter to a frying pan and put it over a medium heat. When the butter is foaming lightly, add the shallots and garlic. After a couple of minutes, pour in a glass of wine and the remaining lemon juice. Allow the liquid to reduce by half, then take the pan off the heat and add the reserved diced butter. Using a fork or whisk, agitate the contents of the pan until everything emulsifies into a velvety sauce.

Stir in the parsley, season, then remove from the heat.

Pull the lobster meat from the shells. Cut it into chunks and drop these into the rich, buttery sauce. Do the same with the claw meat. Serve in the lobster shell.

Pour everybody a glass of wine and eat noisily and messily with your fingers, toasting the noble creature that made this possible.

OYSTERS ROCKEFELLER

Serves 4 as a starter   *months with a r in them*

Named after the president of Standard Oil, who in his day was the richest man in the world, this is the only way I like cooked oysters. Generally I consider the cooking of the magnificent oyster a crime against nature, but done like this I don't mind. This is easy and works great on a barbecue.

As with any oyster you eat, smell each one after it is opened and, of course, if the oyster is not welded shut when you handle it, it is off and may cause appalling two-way complications, so ditch it!

12 oysters in the shell, fresh and alive (see introduction)
100g/3½oz/scant ½ cup unsalted
    butter, plus a little extra for finishing
2 shallots, peeled and finely chopped
1 clove of garlic, peeled and finely
    chopped
1 stick (stalk) of celery, finely chopped
1 tbsp finely chopped flat-leaf parsley
100g/3½oz fresh spinach, roughly
    chopped
a splash of Pernod
100g/3½oz/scant 1 cup breadcrumbs,
    ideally Panko (see page 46)
sea salt and freshly ground black pepper

Open the oysters, discard the top shell and loosen the meat. Set them aside in the shell, covered and in the fridge, keeping them in their juice.

Melt the butter in a heavy pan over a medium heat and add the shallots, garlic, celery and parsley. Fry for 2 minutes. Add the spinach and cook until wilted. Pour in a splash of Pernod and flame, then season.

Preheat the grill to medium. Pop a spoonful of the Rockefeller mixture onto each oyster. Sprinkle each one with breadcrumbs. Top with a small dot of butter and nestle the oyster onto rock salt. Grill for 3 minutes, then serve with chilled white Burgundy.

RIVER FISH

RIVER FISH

To most of us in the UK, the idea of eating river fish is slightly odd. We eat salmon and trout, obviously, but if I brought a big gleaming pike around to your house, you'd think I'd gone off my rocker. On the Continent I would be welcomed with open arms, for once you get past the bones, there is some very fine flesh on a pike.

I think this reluctance is because we are a nation of coarse anglers, to whom the fish is sacred, and a jolly fine notion that is too, for it guarantees a healthy river system with plenty of fish. Personally, I love to cook a nice river fish now and then, and if I am fishing in a place that allows it, then I am only too delighted to take a few fat perch or a pike home. The perch is my favourite, being rather like a freshwater sea bass, with beautiful sweet flesh and a lovely firm texture. But eating a trout caught scant hours earlier on the side of a wild river, with the scent of woodsmoke drifting across the wind, is deeply evocative and must be done; all you need is butter, lemons, foil and a sense of adventure!

When contemplating cooking a river fish that you've caught yourself, always look at the water it has come from. If you have caught your perch or pike in a muddy, slightly urban stretch of river, then think twice about eating it. A fish can taste muddy if it has lived its life in a muddy environment, which is a typical problem with lake trout. Try to eat fish from faster-moving water – the chalk streams of southern England are clear and swift and the fish found within them taste delicious.

In Britain, we focus mainly on eating the big three river fish: salmon, trout and sea trout. Simple, you would have thought, but there are many factors to consider when choosing your fish.

Salmon is probably the most-consumed fish in the UK. It is full of omega 3 oils and all sorts of other goodies. The Atlantic salmon is a miraculous fish. It is anadromous, which simply means it starts life in a river, then goes to sea to grow (sometimes for years), then returns to its river of birth to spawn. This is when it's traditionally caught, originally by line and fly, as it continues its amazing journey up wild European rivers. In recent years, fishing at sea and heavy drift netting has reduced numbers catastrophically.

Thankfully, huge efforts by conservation groups have meant that wild salmon stocks are showing signs of recovery. A good example is the river Tyne which, 30 years ago, was an horrifically polluted waterway full of industrial effluent. Last year, the Tyne and its tributaries were the most prolific salmon rivers in England. Fishermen are learning to return the female and mature fish alive to continue their journey, and only to take the young males, known as grilse.

This does mean that wild salmon is prohibitively expensive, thus making good farmed salmon the best that most of us can buy. My favourite is the sea-farmed and organic Glenarm brand, which has the muscle tone and colour of a wild fish and has been farmed offshore, thus not polluting any sea lochs with their effluent.

Trout can be either the native brown or the non-native rainbow varieties, and will usually be farmed. Look for good fins that are not battered, indicating a high standard of aquaculture.

Sea trout are a brown trout that has become anadromous and gone to sea to feed and grow. Hugely prized by anglers, these fish are hard to catch and incredibly delicious.

SALMON WITH SOY, GINGER AND RED PEPPERS

Serves 4   *All year round*

This recipe has been influenced by my visits to the Pacific coast of Canada, where salmon is an essential part of the diet and Asian influences abound. Wild salmon is such a firm and flavoursome fish that it can take the strong flavours involved. If you are using farmed salmon, try to use good-quality organic, offshore-farmed salmon, of which several brands are available. This can be cooked on the barbecue but will also work very well under a grill.

juice and zest of 2 limes
50ml/2fl oz/¼ cup soy sauce
1 tbsp maple syrup
a large piece of fresh root ginger, peeled
1 x 1kg/2¼lb centre-cut piece of
    salmon fillet

2 red (bell) peppers, deseeded and
    finely sliced
1 bulb of fennel, finely sliced
1 tbsp vegetable oil
sea salt and freshly ground black pepper

In a small bowl, mix half the lime juice and all the zest with the soy sauce and maple syrup. Grate half the ginger into the liquid, then transfer it to a pan and cook it over a medium heat until it has reduced to a sticky glaze. Paint the salmon fillet with the glaze and leave, covered in the fridge, to marinate for half an hour.

Meanwhile, in a separate bowl, mix the red (bell) peppers and fennel with the oil. Cut the remaining ginger into very fine julienne and add it to the vegetables. Transfer the mixture to a pan and cook it over a medium heat for 4–7 minutes. Remove from the heat, squeeze the remaining lime juice over the vegetables and then season with salt and pepper.

Preheat the grill to high. Grill the salmon for 10 minutes, turning it halfway through, until evenly cooked. Just before it is done, give it a final brush with any remaining glaze. Serve on a large dish surrounded by the pepper, fennel and ginger mixture.

CURED SALMON WITH FENNEL AND LEMON

Serves 12 (one side of salmon will serve 10–20 people, depending how hungry you are)
March to September

Fish was the earliest form of protein to be cured or preserved. This is no doubt due to the speed with which it goes off. Typical methods of preserving fish include air-drying (still popular in Scandinavia and northwestern Canada), smoking and salting. Modern smoked salmon is merely salt-cured fish that has then been flavoured with smoke – the real preserving work has been done by the salt, and possibly sugar, used to dry out and cure the fish.

This recipe is a variation on gravadlax, which we all know and love. Gravadlax translates from Swedish into 'cured salmon'. Essentially, we are carrying out the first phase of smoked salmon, but leaving out the smoke, and flavouring instead with fennel and lemon.

500g/1lb 2oz table salt
400g/14oz/2 cups caster (superfine) sugar
2 handfuls of fennel fronds
1 tbsp black peppercorns
zest of 2 unwaxed lemons
1 side of salmon, ideally very fresh, top-quality, organic, farmed salmon
 (if you can get wild salmon, terrific, but try to avoid netted salmon)

Put the salt, sugar and fennel in a food processor. Grind up the black peppercorns in a pestle and mortar until they are reasonably fine, then add to the food processor. Whizz for 30 seconds, pour it into a deep roasting tin (pan) and add the lemon zest.

To prepare the salmon, cut off the fatty edge of the fillet with a sharp knife and make sure that all the pin bones are removed. Nestle the fillet into the salt and sugar mixture, then heap handfuls of it over the fish, making sure it is well covered. Cover loosely with clingfilm (plastic wrap) and leave in the fridge for 12 hours.

Turn the fillet, re-cover it and put it back in the fridge for another 12 hours. Lots of the brine will turn into an oily, herby liquor. Turn, re-cover one more time and leave for a further 12 hours, so that the fish has a total of 36 hours in the mixture.

Remove the fish and rinse briefly under a tap to remove the excess salt and sugar. Pat dry with paper towels, place on a wire rack and put in the fridge, uncovered, for 4 hours (put it at the top of the fridge so no other foods can drip on it).

Slice the cured salmon thinly at a diagonal. Serve with a salad of rocket and shaved fennel, dressed with lemon juice and extra-virgin olive oil. If you like, mix mayonnaise with wholegrain mustard, lemon juice and chopped fennel fronds to make a sauce.

POACHED SEA TROUT WITH MARSH SAMPHIRE AND LEMON BUTTER

Serves 4   *March to October*

The sea trout is one of our finest tasting fish and yet is often overshadowed by its larger relative, the salmon. Sea trout are anadromous, which means they can switch to living in salt water to fresh water and back again. Essentially, a sea trout is a brown trout that has decided to leave the river and go to sea to feed, then return to its native river to spawn. If you can find a sea trout at the fishmonger's, do buy one, especially if they have a good-sized fish of 1.8–2.7kg/4–6lb. Because this will be a wild fish, the flavour will be exquisite and the texture delicate, so let's not muck around with it too much. Poaching is an excellent technique, as it retains all the flavour within the fish.

1 x 1.8–2.7kg/4–6lb sea trout,
    scaled, gutted, filleted (skin on)
    and pin-boned

For the bouillon
2 litres/3½ pints/8½ cups water
2 bay leaves
12 black peppercorns
1 lemon, halved
1 bulb of fennel, quartered
1 tbsp sea salt

For the lemon butter
250g/9oz/1¼ cups butter
1 shallot, peeled and very finely chopped
juice of 2 lemons
sea salt and freshly ground black pepper

For the samphire
250g/9oz marsh samphire
a large knob of butter

Cut the sea trout fillets into four large pieces, removing the tail end – which you will cook and eat greedily on your own at a later date. For the bouillon, pour the water into a large, not-too-deep pan, then add the bay leaves, peppercorns, lemon, fennel and sea salt (don't squeeze the lemon; just float it in the water).

Carefully immerse the fish, skin-side up, in the bouillon and bring the water temperature to about 70°C/158°F. Immediately turn off the heat; when the fish feels firm to the touch, it is ready – this should take about 6 minutes.

For the lemon butter, bring a quarter of the butter to foaming point in a small pan over a low-medium heat. Add the shallot and soften for 2 minutes. Squeeze in the lemon juice and add the rest of the butter, whisking. Take off the heat and season.

Two minutes before you are ready to eat, pour boiling water over the samphire, then drain and toss in a little butter and black pepper. Divide among four plates. Lay one poached piece of fish on top of the samphire, then surround with lemon butter.

POACHED SEA TROUT WITH SPINACH AND HOLLANDAISE

Serves 4   *March to October*

The sea trout is the greatest prize of the fly fisherman; indeed, I have spent many frustrating evenings (and nights) fishing for these elusive creatures in the wilder parts of Wales, in whose rivers they abound (and where they are referred to as *sewin*). I prefer the taste of a sea trout to any other freshwater fish – they are meaty, firm-fleshed and should be cooked very simply.

1 x 2.7–3.6kg/6–8lb sea trout, scaled, gutted and cut into steaks

For the spinach
200g/7oz spinach or 2 black cabbage, shredded
a small knob of butter
sea salt and freshly ground black pepper

For the bouillon
2 litres/3½ pints/8½ cups water
1 bulb of fennel, quartered
6 black peppercorns

1 shallot, peeled and halved
2 sticks (stalks) of celery, chopped
½ lemon
1 tbsp sea salt

For the hollandaise
2 tbsp white wine
1 shallot, peeled and finely chopped
3 tbsp white-wine vinegar
juice of 1 large lemon
3 medium egg yolks
250g/9oz/1¼ cups butter, melted but not hot
sea salt and white pepper

For the bouillon, pour the water into a large, not-too-deep pan, then add the fennel, peppercorns, shallot, celery, lemon and salt. Bring to a simmer, then turn off the heat.

There are quick and easy ways to make hollandaise using a processor or stick blender, but sometimes it is nicer to do things by hand. Put the wine, shallot, vinegar and lemon juice into a pan over a medium heat and reduce by two-thirds. Strain the liquid through a sieve. Tip the egg yolks into a heatproof bowl and add the strained liquor. Set this bowl over a pan of simmering water and whisk vigorously until you create a frothy, light mixture. Take the bowl off the heat and pour in the warm melted butter, whisking all the time. The sauce will thicken steadily until it has a creamy consistency. Season with salt and white pepper. (If you wish to add flavour, you can add chopped fresh herbs such as tarragon or coriander [cilantro]). Keep the hollandaise warm over a bowl of warm water while you cook the sea trout.

Lay the sea trout steaks in the hot bouillon and poach for 10 minutes until firm. Cook the spinach or cabbage leaves in boiling water for 5 minutes, drain and toss with butter. Season and serve alongside the fish with the hollandaise poured over the top.

BROWN TROUT IN FOIL WITH CHILLI-GARLIC MAYONNAISE

Serves 2 *March to October*

I first cooked this recipe on a fabulous day filming *Countrywise Kitchen* in the beautiful Lake District. We had met Lee Cummings, a brilliant fly-fisherman, who had agreed to show me one of his favourite waters set in gobsmacking scenery in the high Lakes, Devoke Tarn, which is England's highest trout fishery. As so often happens when filming, the weather gods were not being forthcoming – it was cold, grey and a cruel east wind was blowing. No matter what outdoor food-gathering activity you are doing, there is a common hatred of an east wind! In this instance, it stopped the insects from hatching and prevented the trout from rising to the fly. I have always been a fly-fisherman and the main requirement for success is perseverance, so that's what we did. Eventually we triumphed: Lee with a good brown trout of about 350g/12oz, and me with a perch, which while ignored culinarily by us Brits, is revered on the Continent as a sort of freshwater sea bass. A sheltered spot was found, a small fire kindled and we retired to our well-earned lunch...

2 lemons, thinly sliced
100g/3½oz/½ cup butter
2 brown trout or perch, scaled, gutted
   and cleaned
125ml/4fl oz/1 glass of dry white
   wine, such as Sancerre
sea salt and freshly ground black pepper

For the mayonnaise
juice of ½ lemon
1 tbsp white wine vinegar
a pinch of saffron strands
1 medium egg yolk
250ml/9fl oz/1 cup vegetable oil
1 tbsp finely sliced chives
1 hot red chilli (chile), finely chopped
1 clove of garlic, peeled and grated

For the mayonnaise, squeeze the lemon into a large bowl, add the vinegar, saffron and egg yolk and whisk vigorously, pouring in a very thin trickle of oil. Keep adding the oil until the mayonnaise is the required consistency (I like it quite runny); if you want it stiffer, you will need more oil. Mix in the chives, chilli (chili) and garlic, season and leave in the fridge, covered, for the chilli to heat things up.

Light the barbecue and let the flames die down so the coals are grey-hot. For the fish, lay three 30sq cm/12sq inch sheets of foil on the ground. Place a row of lemon slices along the middle of each sheet. Dot these with butter, then lay the fish on top. Season and lay more lemon slices over that (this will stop the fish skin sticking to the foil and protect it from the heat). Sprinkle with half the wine and drink the rest. Cover with the second layer of foil and form into an envelope; seal the edges.

continues overleaf >

Bash down the fire so that embers remain and fold the remaining piece of foil in half. Lay this on the embers, lay the envelope of fish on top and leave it for 10 minutes.

When it's done, open the envelope, remove the lemon and lay the fish onto plates with a generous dollop of mayo. Drink a crispy Sancerre with this.

BARBECUED BROWN TROUT FILLETS WITH WATERCRESS

Serves 4   *March to September*

Surely there is no finer place to fish for the elusive trout than on the river where fly-fishing started – the River Test in Hampshire. I was fortunate enough to fly-fish on one of the Test tributaries for *Countrywise Kitchen* during the magic fortnight of the mayfly. This two-to-three week period is the single most important time in the wild trout's calendar. They pack on a lot of weight for very little effort, since the mayflies come in their millions and are a pretty decent mouthful.

I was upstream, dry-fly-fishing using a mayfly imitation, and succeeded to my amazement in hooking two wild brown trout for the camera. Catching or shooting things to order for a TV crew is seriously tricky, so when it all works, it is fabulous. To cap it all, my faithful hound, Sassy, waded the whole river with me – hoping, I think, that the trout would turn into deer.

The fly-fishing tradition on the Test and other rivers is fantastic for the environment – fishermen pay to fish these waters and the money goes directly into the ongoing conservation efforts of the river-owners.

The key to this little dish is in neatly filleting the fish, then grilling them in one of those wire mesh sandwich grills that you buy for doing toast on an Aga – an invaluable tool! Serve the trout with aioli (see page 88) and piles of fresh watercress; a real treat on a Spring day.

1 x 3lb/1.4kg brown trout, scaled, gutted and cleaned
2 tbsp olive oil
1 lemon
sea salt and freshly ground black pepper

To serve
2 bunches of Hampshire watercress
a bowl of aioli (see page 88)

Light the barbecue and let the flames die down so the coals are grey-hot. Fillet the fish; you can get your fishmonger to do this, but it is good to learn to do it yourself. Place the fish with its backbone facing you and the head to the left. Using a long thin knife, make a cut through the flesh just below the gills round to the backbone, then insert the knife between the flesh and the ribs and cut down one side of the spine, keeping the knife close to the bone. Keeping the blade flat and the fish anchored with your left hand, cut all the way down to the tail, then remove the fillet. Turn the fish over and do the same on the other side, again working from head to tail, then remove the bones in one fluid cut.

Pour half the oil over the trout fillets and rub it in. Season the fish well with salt and pepper and add a squeeze of lemon juice. Cut each fillet in half crossways, then sandwich the four half-fillets in the wire mesh Aga toaster and cook over white coals for 5 minutes skin-side down, then turn over and finish for 3 or 4 minutes. (Alternatively cook under a medium-hot grill until done.)

Dress the watercress with the remaining lemon juice and olive oil and serve with the fish together with a dollop of aioli.

CRAYFISH SOUP

Serves 6–10   *May to September*

Signal crayfish were introduced into Britain in the 1970s, mainly to help farmers diversify and look for other means of making an income. The crayfish, *Pacifastacus leniusculus*, is originally an American species, extremely adaptable, very hardy, large, voracious and all-consuming of aquatic life in its path. This invader has done very, very well in Britain. It came to our shores from America via Sweden. In Sweden, crayfish are a huge delicacy and much prized; over here, however, they have taken us somewhat by surprise. Unfortunately, the signal crayfish carries a plague (the crayfish plague), which doesn't kill the signal, but does kill our native white-clawed species of crayfish, which has now largely disappeared from southern rivers and lakes.

The good news is that crayfish are very easy to catch. All you need is a mesh trap, which can be bought from most fishing shops or online, a fish head or two, or a punctured can of dog food. (As a point of interest, crayfish prefer dog food in gravy to dog food in jelly.) When a decent-sized trap is left in a deep part of any southern river for 24 hours or so, you should see a haul of 1–2kg/2¼–4½lb of crayfish. On occasion I have pulled up over 10kg/22lb in one night, when the traps were lowered into a new spot of water.

Once cleaned up, these shellfish are delicious and, while fiddly to prepare, are really worth the effort. It takes a bit of doing, but I believe it is the equal of any lobster, crab or langoustine beast I have eaten.

2kg/4½lb live signal crayfish
100ml/3½fl oz/scant ½ cup extra-virgin olive oil
12 cloves of garlic, peeled
3 bulbs of fennel, roughly chopped
6 sticks (stalks) of celery, roughly chopped
2 carrots, roughly chopped
3 onions, peeled and roughly chopped
a large pinch of the best saffron you can buy
2 x 400g cans chopped plum tomatoes
1kg/2¼lb fresh ripe cherry tomatoes
175ml/6fl oz/scant 1 cup dry white wine
2 litres/3½ pints/8½ cups fish stock
juice of 1 lemon
25ml/1fl oz/1 shot of Pastis (Pernod)
25ml/1fl oz/1 shot of Cognac
sea salt and freshly ground black pepper

continues overleaf >

Run your live crayfish under a tap or a shower-head for 5 minutes to remove any dirt. (If they've been in a chalk-stream environment, they won't need too much cleaning.) Put them in the freezer for half an hour to dull their nervous systems.

You will need a large casserole pan and a very large boiling pan or stockpot. Fill this second pan with water and bring to the boil. Boil the crayfish in batches for 10 minutes at a time, then remove and plunge into iced water. Once all your crayfish are cooked and refreshed, pull all the claws and tails off, and discard their heads (they are muddy and they don't taste great).

Heat up the oil in the casserole over a low–medium heat. Throw in the garlic, fennel, celery, carrots and onions and sweat for 20 minutes. Add the saffron, all the tomatoes, the wine and crayfish tails and claws – shells and meat. Pour in the fish stock and squeeze in the lemon. Bring to the boil, then simmer for 20 minutes.

Grind up everything, one batch at a time, in a food processor or with a large, powerful hand blender. Using two layers of muslin (cheesecloth), strain the soup though the muslin and a sieve into a second container. This will take time, it is boring and very messy, but the result is worth it. Once you are left with a clear, saffron-coloured liquor, discard the pulp, having a good final squeeze to remove as much as possible of the content.

Pour this liquor into a pan, put it over a medium heat, uncovered, and reduce it by half – this will concentrate the flavours magnificently. Season until you have a wonderful deep-flavoured crayfish soup. Finish with a shot each of Pastis (Pernod) and Cognac.

Classically, this dish is served with rouille or garlic and chilli mayonnaise (see page 134), croûtons and grated Gruyère cheese.

SMOKED EEL SOUP

Serves 8   *All year round*

Smoked eels are to be valued. These deliciously fatty fish have made one of the world's great journeys to arrive on your plate: from our rivers to the Sargasso Sea and back. The eel has declined dramatically in numbers in recent years, so when you buy yours from the fishmonger, or order it over the internet, make sure it comes from an accredited and sustainable supply. Brilliant simply eaten on brown bread with mayonnaise, the eel gives off its best when made into this delightfully light and smoky soup, which is incredibly easy to make.

4 medium onions, peeled and sliced
75g/3oz/6 tbsp butter
2 medium celeriac (celery root), peeled
    and cut into cubes
1 litre/1¾ pints/4¼ cups chicken stock

500ml/17fl oz/generous 2 cups milk
6 bay leaves
1 smoked eel, skinned and cut into
    4 pieces
sea salt and freshly ground black pepper

Sweat the onions in the butter in a heavy pan over a medium heat until they are soft and translucent. Add the celeriac, cover with the stock and milk, then add the bay leaves. Bring up to simmering point, reduce the heat to medium-low, and add the pieces of smoked eel.

Simmer until the celeriac is tender (about 40 minutes), then remove the eel and pull the meat off the bone.

Put the meat back into the soup, fish out the bay leaves and blend the soup until fine. Check the seasoning, adding salt and pepper if necessary.

CHEESE AND MILK

CHEESE AND MILK

The French famously boast that they have a different cheese for every day of the year. Quite a statement, and certainly they have some awesome cheeses, but us *rosbifs* are challenging their reign as Europe's cheese royalty. Every month I get information about a new cheese that has won awards for taste and character. Our artisan cheese-makers make some of the best cheese in the world.

Really good cheese is a labour of love. We Brits are, of course, famous for two cheeses: Stilton and Cheddar; but there are many more. One cheese that plays a part in this book is a creamy, sometimes stinking work of art called Waterloo (see page 148). This cheese is made next to the Duke of Wellington's estate, hence the name, and is like butter crossed with clotted Jersey cream. The problem, as with so many artisan cheeses, is that it is made in small amounts by cheese professionals, so getting it can be tricky.

A lot of our finest cheese is not the result of the humble dairy cow. The UK is home to producers of some of the finest goats cheese around – I filmed some beautiful Guernsey goats whose milk produced a stunning cottage-style cheese. Now, I am well known for my dislike of goats cheese, so this was a tricky old shoot for me, but the cottage cheese was lovely, with not a hint of goatiness. However, the same cheese, left for six months, was a different story – with a powerful flavour of goat, it was a good example of what the simple process of time can do to a food. Whatever cheese you buy, think about the effort that goes into making it. Some cheeses have to be matured quite literally for years to reach their peak, so think twice before casually using it in cooking or melting it.

We British also produce stunning cream and butter that I have not seen rivalled anywhere. Try double Jersey or Guernsey cream – glorious-yellow and so thick that you need a spoon to get it out of the pot – or that amazing Cornish clotted cream, with a crust a quarter of an inch thick. Spoon it over a steaming warm scone, then pile it high with rich raspberry jam, and... well, you get the idea.

BUCKLEBURY RAREBIT

Serves 2   *All year round*

I love cheese on toast, and I suspect that I am not alone. In its natural form it is a winner, but this little variation is something I have been snacking on for as long as I can remember. Due to the addition of Worcestershire sauce it has similarities to Welsh rarebit, but since my only connection to Wales was a stint at university there, I have named it after the village of my birth and where my family still lives: Bucklebury in Berkshire. This recipe calls for really good, strong Cheddar that is properly mature. I like 24-month-old Montgomery Cheddar; it crumbles and is really tangy.

1 tbsp vegetable oil
1 large onion, peeled and finely sliced
1 clove of garlic, peeled and finely chopped
2 sprigs of thyme, leaves picked
2 large slices of white or brown farmhouse bread
1 tbsp Worcestershire sauce
200g/7oz good strong Cheddar, thinly sliced
freshly ground black pepper, to taste

Heat the vegetable oil in a heavy pan over a very low heat. Throw in the onions and cook for 5–10 minutes to start to soften them. Add the garlic and thyme leaves and cook for a further 15 minutes; you want the onion and garlic to have melted down completely and to have taken on a lovely caramel colour.

Preheat the grill to high, then toast the bread on both sides until it is golden. Spoon the onion mixture evenly over both pieces of toast and sprinkle a few drops of Worcestershire sauce over each. Lay the cheese over the onions, covering the toast completely. Sprinkle with more Worcestershire sauce and grind plenty of black pepper over the top. Grill until bubbling, brown and melting. I love to eat this in front of the telly with a cold Guinness.

PEPPERY LEAF SALAD WITH GOATS CHEESE DRESSING

Serves 4 as a side salad   *May to September*

Summer is a time to be inventive with salads. Rocket, mizuna and frisée are all among my favourite salad leaves. This goats cheese dressing is simple to make, yet strong enough to deal with the powerful flavour of the leaves. If you wish to make this salad more of a main meal, add croûtons and possibly shavings of Parmesan.

a large bowl of washed mixed leaves, ideally
    rocket, mizuna and watercress

For the dressing
1 tsp Dijon mustard
1 tsp runny honey
juice of 1 large lemon
1 tbsp cider vinegar
150ml/5fl oz/scant ⅔ cup vegetable oil
50ml/2fl oz/¼ cup extra-virgin olive oil
100g/3½oz soft goats cheese, rind removed
sea salt and freshly ground black pepper

To make the dressing, mix the mustard, honey, lemon juice and vinegar together in a bowl using a whisk, then add both oils. Whisk well, then crumble or spoon in the goats cheese (depending on whether it is soft and crumbly or soft and gooey). Mix thoroughly with a hand blender until you have a creamy, rich dressing. Taste and add seasoning if you wish.

Toss the salad leaves in 2–3 tablespoons of the dressing. I find this is a brilliant side salad with a simply roasted chicken. The dressing works well over new potatoes.

BAKED WATERLOO OR CAMEMBERT WITH APRICOTS AND ROSEMARY

Serves 4 as a main (more as a starter)   *All year round*

Ever since my days of living in the Alps, I have had a love affair with melted cheese. Fondues, tartiflettes... you name it, I love it. British cheese-makers are now rivalling the French in artisan cheese production, and nowhere is this more the case than with my favourite cheese, Waterloo. This cheese (named after an incident the French would rather forget) is creamy, better than any Camembert I have eaten, and made in such small quantities that it is difficult to get hold of. Waterloo and its ewe's milk sister, Wigmore, are perfectly suited to the decadent method of cooking employed in this recipe. This recipe was invented by Jonathan Taylor, head chef at my pub, The Pot Kiln. The idea is to bake the cheese in a puff pastry crust, so that when you cut it open and fall upon its molten contents with chunks of bread and crunchy pieces of vegetables, it is like opening a present. It makes perfect Winter party food.

1 x 450g/1lb Waterloo/Wigmore or Camembert
3 cloves of garlic, peeled and cut into small slices
2 sprigs of rosemary
100g/3½oz dried apricots, ideally Hunza, sliced
500g/1lb 2oz good-quality puff pastry
plain (all-purpose) flour, to dust
2 eggs, beaten, for the egg-wash
sea salt and freshly ground black pepper
crusty bread, to serve
batons of carrots, cucumber and red pepper, to serve

Preheat the oven to 200°C/400°F/gas mark 6. Line a baking tray (sheet) with baking parchment. Stud the top of the cheese with the garlic slices. Remove the leaves from the sprigs of rosemary and stud the cheese with them, too. Sprinkle the apricot slices over the top of the cheese, then sprinkle with salt and pepper.

Roll out the pastry on a lightly floured surface into two discs, one slightly larger than the cheese and one 10cm/4 inches larger than that. Lay the cheese on the smaller disc, then place the larger disc over the top. Crimp the edges to make a neat domed parcel. Paint thoroughly with the egg-wash, then score whatever decorative pattern you wish to on top of the pastry and paint with the egg-wash again.

Place on the prepared tray and bake for 20 minutes, until golden brown. Place the cooked cheese in the centre of a large serving plate. Surround with crusty white bread and batons of crunchy vegetables. Serve with ice-cold Champagne or Muscadet.

STILTON CHEESE MOUSSE

Serves 10 as a starter   *All year round*

One of my main culinary handicaps is my inability to eat blue cheese – I so wish I could, for Stilton is surely one of our national treasures. This iconic cheese is produced in only three counties: Derbyshire, Nottinghamshire and Leicestershire, and just six dairies in the country make it. It has its own certification trademark and is an EU-protected food name.

   This dish is very easy to make and, most importantly, it really brings out the character of the cheese.

200ml/7fl oz/scant 1 cup milk
200g/7oz Stilton
a pinch of salt
1½ leaves of gelatine
200ml/7fl oz/scant 1 cup double (heavy) cream
200ml/7fl oz/scant 1 cup whipping cream
pieces of apple, celery or pear, to serve

Pour the milk into a medium-sized saucepan and bring it up to a simmer. Crumble the Stilton in and stir gently until it is melted. Add the salt.

Strain the cheese and milk mix through a sieve into a bowl. Add the gelatine, then nestle the bowl into a larger bowl of ice to cool. After a couple of minutes, stir the mixture well to make sure the gelatine is fully mixed in.

Mix the double and whipping creams together in a bowl and whisk to soft peaks. Add half the cream to the cheese mixture and stir to combine, then fold in the rest to form a light, smooth mousse. Pour the mixture into ramekins, cover and chill until needed. Serve with raw apple, celery and pear.

WINTER REBLOCHON PASTIES

Makes 6 pasties   *Winter*

I lived in the French Alps for many years, where the simple and rather pungent cheese reblochon was almost a religion. Its most famous use is in the iconic dish tartiflette, which is living proof that you cannot have too much in the way of bacon, cheese, potatoes and onions. I have Anglicised the dish and made it portable with these pasties. They're delicious, if dangerous when the molten cheese comes oozing out. For those of you who have not tried reblochon, I urge you to have a go – it has an astonishing flavour, especially when melted.

2 tbsp vegetable oil
2 onions, peeled and thinly sliced
2 cloves of garlic, peeled and thinly sliced
150g/5oz smoked back (Canadian)
   bacon, diced
200g/7oz unpeeled baby new potatoes,
   boiled until just cooked, cut into
   large dice
2 leeks, finely sliced
1 bunch of thyme, leaves picked

75ml/3fl oz/⅓ cup dry white wine
500g/1lb 2oz good-quality puff pastry,
   rolled out to 5mm/¼-inch thick
plain (all-purpose) flour, to dust
2 eggs, beaten, for egg-wash
100ml/3½fl oz/scant ½ cup double
   (heavy) cream
1 reblochon (as smelly as possible), sliced
sea salt and freshly ground black pepper

Preheat the oven to 200°C/400°F/gas mark 6. Line a baking tray (sheet) with some baking parchment.

Put a heavy pan on a fairly high heat, add the oil and fry the onions and garlic. Once they are showing signs of browning, add the bacon and cook for 5 minutes. If you need more oil, add some. Add the cooked potatoes and the leeks and cook for 5 minutes, then add the thyme and wine and cook for 1 more minute. Let the mixture cool down.

Roll out the pastry on a lightly floured surface into six 15cm/6-inch discs and brush the edges with egg-wash. Spoon a little of the mixture into the centre of each pastry disc and sprinkle with salt and pepper. Add a splash of cream and a couple of slices of reblochon to each and close the pasties, crimping the join securely. Brush well with egg-wash, transfer to the baking tray and bake for 20 minutes.

MUSHROOMS

MUSHROOMS

Britain probably has Europe's most perfect climate for encouraging the growth of wild mushrooms. Generally moist with plenty of woodland, it is a great breeding ground for magical fungi. Trying to write a guide to mushrooms is not my goal in this book, but a few words of advice may be helpful.

Mushroom-hunting in the UK started a long time ago. Edible wild mushrooms have always been a staple of hunter-gatherers, and I am certain that our ancestors were experts on what, and what not, to eat.

The advent of convenience foods, the post-war change in eating habits and the loss of rural skills has meant that, until recently, mushroom-gathering was a dark and nearly forgotten art.

I have spent hundreds of hours in the woods in Berkshire foraging for these elusive gems, and when stalking or shooting in the Autumn I always have one eye tuned to the ground, marking likely mushroom spots for further investigation. Treat hunting for mushrooms like a military operation, and employ the art of reconnaisance; it will not be wasted. I go so far as to mark on a map where and what I find, on the principle that we will almost certainly find the same thing in the same place the next year.

The main hunting season is the Autumn – the hunt begins when the leaves turn golden and the days shorten. Buttery yellow chanterelles, bulbous ceps and huge chicken of the woods, turn people like me into excited wrecks. But Autumn is not the only time; there are some Spring mushrooms that are amazing and sought-after too. One of the most common Spring mushrooms is the St George's mushroom, which grows in fairy rings all over the southern British downland, classically around St George's day – 23rd April. I love using them in April and May, and you cannot easily mistake them for anything else! The other major Spring species is the morel, which is easily identified by its brain like form. It is one of the world's best mushrooms, and is especially good dried.

What you need before you go mushroom-hunting is knowledge. Buy a good mushroom book. To my mind, you cannot beat books by the great Roger Phillips; they are photographic and unparallelled in clarity. The problem is that mushrooms do not conform in shape and colour, so to be certain you are really on the right track, go out with an expert or go on a course. I tend to stick to bombproof, easy-to-identify mushrooms that I feel totally safe about serving to my guests, and that have amazing edible qualities. The ones I use most often are: ceps, wood blewits, hedgehog fungus, field mushrooms, amethyst deceivers, chanterelles, winter chanterelles, giant puffballs and chicken of the woods.

These are all very common, easy to identify, and are hard to mistake for anything really poisonous. Don't forget that while we do not have many really dodgy mushrooms, the deadly ones, such as death caps and panther cap, are fatal. So take your time, do not pick anything you are not sure of, and cook them gently. Lastly, never wash a wild mushroom: brush it with a soft brush instead; otherwise it will turn into a soggy wreck.

A BERKSHIRE SPRING SALAD

Serves 2 *May/June*

This is a light, fresh Spring salad that I made after a morning out in the Berkshire woods last year. Just because a dish does not include leafy bits does not mean it can't be a salad. The key here is to use one of late Spring's most fabulous ingredients: the baby broad bean. You should be able to cook and eat a broad bean without peeling it. As soon as you feel you have to peel them, do not use them for this dish. Also included are fresh herbs and the young *pied de mouton* (or hedgehog mushrooms) that start emerging in the woods at this time. For the poached egg, I always try to use a pheasant's egg, but if that's not possible, a small fresh hen's egg will do fine.

150g/5oz broad (fava) beans
150g/5oz small hedgehog mushrooms
100ml/3½fl oz/scant ½ cup olive oil
juice of 1 lemon
a small handful of flat-leaf parsley
6 mint leaves
1 small bunch of chives, finely chopped
2 pheasant's or hen's eggs
1 tbsp white-wine vinegar
2 small handfuls of frisée lettuce
sea salt and freshly ground black pepper

Cook the broad beans in boiling salted water for 2 minutes, then refresh in iced water and set aside. In a frying pan, gently cook the mushrooms in a tablespoon or so of olive oil until they just colour. Remove from the pan and place them to one side, too.

Whizz up the remaining olive oil, the lemon juice, parsley and mint in a blender to create a fine green sauce. Add the chives and season to taste with salt and pepper.

Poach the eggs in water with a little vinegar added (see page 172).

Now return the mushrooms and broad beans to the frying pan and warm them ever so gently. Stir in a tablespoon of the green sauce. Dress the frisée lettuce with a little of the green sauce and place a pile in the centre of each plate. Spoon the mushrooms and beans around the frisée and gently place a poached egg on top of each pile. A final drizzle of green sauce can be added atop the egg if artistic licence requires it.

DEVILLED WILD MUSHROOMS ON TOAST

Serves 4   *Late Summer/Autumn*

This recipe would have struck a chord with any upper-class Victorian. Those folk would 'devill' anything, from kidneys to mushrooms, spicing it up if they possibly could. Devilled kidneys, specifically, are making a real comeback on gastro pub menus. The 'devilling' part simply refers to a piquant, hot and tangy sauce that really complements the strong flavours of kidneys and wild mushrooms. I particularly love this recipe when done with a basket-full of wild mushrooms freshly picked in the Autumn. Quick and easy to prepare, it will blow the cobwebs away on a cold, damp morning.

Ideally, you want to use a firm, well-flavoured wild mushroom – if you can find a patch of good fresh chanterelles, they are perfect.

100g/3½oz/½ cup butter
2 cloves of garlic, peeled and grated
450g/1lb chanterelles (or field mushrooms cut into chunks)
1 tsp English mustard
1 tbsp tomato ketchup
2 tsp Worcestershire sauce
10 drops of Tabasco or another hot chilli (chili) sauce
200ml/7fl oz/scant 1 cup double (heavy) cream
1 tsp paprika
75ml/2½fl oz/¼ cup dry sherry
juice of 1 lemon
sea salt and freshly ground black pepper, to taste
4 thick slices of chewy, crusty bread, such as ciabatta or sourdough, to serve

Heat a large, heavy frying pan to medium-hot. Add the butter and garlic and toss in the mushrooms. Turning constantly, cook until the mushrooms start to soften (about 5 minutes).

Meanwhile, mix all the remaining ingredients apart from the sherry, lemon juice and bread in a mixing bowl to make a spiced cream mix.

Add the sherry and lemon juice to the mushrooms, then cook to reduce for 30 seconds. Add the spiced cream and reduce until thick. Check for seasoning.

Toast the bread. Place a slice of toast on each plate and spoon the mushrooms on to them. Serve with extremely cold dry Manzanilla sherry.

FIELD MUSHROOMS BAKED WITH CARAMELIZED ONIONS AND STINKING BISHOP

Serves 4   *Late Summer/Autumn*

The field mushroom is the biggest manly, meaty mushroom that there is. Extremely common in our fields throughout the late summer and early Autumn, they are so dense and firm that they lend themselves to baking whole or stuffing. The flavour is strong, earthy and robust.

I am using Stinking Bishop for this recipe, a cheese with a quite phenomenally pungent aroma, made by the great Charles Martell in Dymock, Gloucestershire. Melted over the sticky caramelized onions, this makes a magnificent, if rather strong-smelling, lunchtime treat.

4 large field mushrooms, each about 10cm/4 inches across
50g/2oz/¼ cup butter
2 cloves of garlic, peeled and chopped
2 tbsp vegetable oil
2 large red onions, peeled and finely sliced
1 tbsp chopped thyme leaves, plus extra to finish
200g/7oz Stinking Bishop, chilled
sea salt and freshly ground black pepper

Preheat the oven to 220°F/425°F/gas mark 7. Remove the stalks from the field mushrooms. Melt the butter in your largest, heaviest frying pan over a medium-high heat and add the garlic. Cook for a minute or two, then add the field mushrooms and fry, gill-side down, for 6–7 minutes. Turn them over, give them another 2 minutes, then remove from the pan and set aside.

Add the oil to the pan, then add the onions. Cook on a very low heat for at least 10–15 minutes, until the onions caramelize. Add the thyme, cook for another minute or so, then remove from the pan.

Put the mushrooms in a roasting dish, season, then spoon the onion mixture equally between them and top with slices of chilled Stinking Bishop. Bake in the oven for 10 minutes. Sprinkle with fresh thyme and a twist of black pepper. Serve with a peppery rocket salad.

WILD MUSHROOM AND HERB OMELETTE

Serves 2   *Autumn*

This recipe was the culmination of a particularly memorable day's filming for *Countrywise Kitchen*. A day of hunting for a variety of wild fungi in the gentle beauty of the Malvern Hills had yielded a fabulous haul. We had found mainly one of my favourite culinary mushrooms, the often underrated and very delicious bay boletus. This is an incredibly common mushroom throughout Britain and should be firmly at the top of any budding mycophiles hit list. A few chanterelles and wood blewits and some fabulous free-range eggs made the choice of dishes on the day an obvious one. The key to cooking wonderful fresh mushrooms like these is never to wash them (they soak up water like a sponge and become horrid); just wipe them. Also, don't overcook them, make sure some texture and firmness remain.

200g/7oz mixed wild seasonal British mushrooms
    (chanterelles, ceps, blewits – whatever you can get locally)
100g/3½oz/½ cup salted butter
2 shallots, peeled and finely diced
1 clove of garlic, peeled and finely diced
4 eggs
a handful of flat-leaf parsley, finely chopped
a handful of chervil, finely chopped
200g/7oz mature Cheddar
sea salt and freshly ground black pepper

You will need three main pieces of equipment for this: a large mixing bowl, a good heavy non-stick or cast-iron frying pan and ideally a gas camping stove.

Chop and tear your mushrooms into large pieces (don't finely dice them, they are such rare and wonderful things that we want to be able to identify them within the finished dish).

Warm the pan on the stove over a medium heat and add half the butter. Add the shallots, garlic and mushrooms and cook for 6–7 minutes, until the mushrooms have softened and lost a lot of their moisture.

Meanwhile, beat the eggs vigorously in a mixing bowl and add the herbs. Season with salt and pepper. Turn up the heat under the pan and add more butter if needed (the mushrooms soak up a lot of butter so you may need a little more). Pour the egg mixture into the pan with the mushrooms and shallots.

continues overleaf >

Using a fork, stir the eggs and mushrooms for the first minute or so until a very runny scrambled-egg mixture starts to appear. At this point, leave the mixture to firm up for a minute or so, shake the pan to break the omelette's hold on the bottom, then carefully tip onto a plate, folding the omelette over as you do so. The underside of the omelette should be golden and magnificent.

Now, taking a sharp knife, cut the centre of the omelette open, exposing the gooey mushroomy centre, grate liberal amounts of cheese into the gap and over the omelette and watch it start to melt.

Consume with gusto while sitting on the tailgate of your truck admiring the view, possibly quaffing a glass of cider as you do so, and toasting the noble fungi that have made this possible.

STUFFED CHICKEN LEGS WITH CEPS AND CHANTERELLES

Serves 6   *Autumn*

Ceps and chanterelles are the wild mushrooms I use most widely in the Autumn. There is nothing to beat the thrill of finding a big, fat penny bun lurking in the depths of a southern wood, then a few steps further on, coming across a magic patch of apricot-scented orange chanterelles. It is one of the most exciting forms of hunting I know.

Chicken and mushrooms work really well together, but we tend to neglect the chicken leg. Given the choice, I would eat chicken leg over chicken breast any day of the week; it has more flavour and lends itself beautifully to stuffing. This recipe requires a little more preparation than many others in the book, but it is brilliant for dinner parties and is relatively cheap to make.

6 chicken legs, drumstick and thigh (use legs from fairly small chickens)
200g/7oz minced (ground) chicken
75ml/2½fl oz/generous ¼ cup double (heavy) cream
a pinch of mace
175g/6oz chanterelles, cleaned
50g/2oz/¼ cup butter, plus a little extra for frying the legs
2 cloves of garlic
1 tbsp chopped thyme leaves
sea salt and freshly ground black pepper

For the sauce
24 small shallots, peeled
50g/2oz/¼ cup butter
100g/3½oz smoked bacon, finely chopped
200g/7oz small ceps, quartered
25g/1oz chanterelles, cleaned
1 clove of garlic, peeled and finely chopped
125ml/4fl oz/½ cup dry white wine
100ml/3½fl oz/scant ½ cup double (heavy) cream
1 tbsp chopped thyme leaves

continues overleaf >

Debone the chicken legs and remove the sinews you find inside. Now put to one side, covered, in the fridge. Mix together the minced chicken with the cream, mace and salt and pepper to taste and put to one side, covered, in the fridge.

In a frying pan over a medium heat, sauté the chanterelles in the butter, garlic and thyme for 6-7 minutes. Once the mushrooms are cooked and the moisture has been sweated out of them, remove from the pan and leave to cool.

Chop the cooked chanterelles coarsely. Mix them into the minced chicken mixture, then spoon the mixture into the cavity of each chicken leg. Roll up each chicken leg carefully and wrap it into a watertight sausage with clingfilm (plastic wrap).

Poach the chicken legs in simmering water for 20 minutes, until cooked through (if you use large chicken legs, this will take longer). Allow the chicken to cool. Preheat the oven to 200°C/400°F/gas mark 6.

Now the legs are ready for final cooking. In a heavy pan, melt a knob (pat) of butter and remove the chicken from the clingfilm. Season the legs and brown them in the pan, then place in the oven for 15–20 minutes, until cooked through. While they cook, make the sauce.

In a frying pan over a medium heat, caramelize the shallots in the butter for 5 or 6 minutes. Add the bacon, ceps, chanterelles and garlic and cook for 5–7 minutes, stirring all the time. When the mushrooms are just cooked, deglaze the pan with the wine and pour in the cream. Cook for 2–3 minutes, until the cream is reduced. Sprinkle in the thyme.

Carve the stuffed chicken legs and serve with the delicious cep and chanterelle sauce.

VEGETABLES

VEGETABLES

As I get older I find myself craving fresh produce more and more. I get an almost slavish and anticipatory delight from watching the garden grow over the Spring months leading into Summer. The joy of having to create dishes around what is growing rather than what I can buy on groaning shelves in the supermarket is huge, and challenging.

Growing vegetables has forced me to think seasonally, to use foodstuffs only when they are at their best, and really to make the most of them when they are there.

I am aware that we cannot all grow our own food, but I would urge you at the very least to buy what is in season, and to buy vegetables that you know have been grown in Britain. Supermarkets are doing very good work on this front, but if in doubt, ask where the vegetable was grown.

Another great way to make yourself cook seasonally and British is to sign up to a veg box scheme. This way, a box of assorted and gorgeous produce will arrive on your doorstep every week, and you will have to be creative to get the most out of it. Remember, if in doubt, make soup!

Growing your own really is an option, even if you have no garden. I have friends in London who have developed window boxes and roof gardens into an art form – it is amazing how many carrots, beetroots and salads three or four good-size window boxes can produce.

It isn't just cultivated vegetables that I love cooking. A lot of wild salad leaves, vegetables and fruit are out there for the picking. Wild garlic grows almost everywhere and is unmistakable (see pages 174, 176 and 190); elderflowers are out in early summer all over Britain and make amazing cordial. If you live by the coast you can graze on samphire, purslane and sea beet, all of which are incredibly good for you.

We tend to go most badly wrong in the Winter, by which I mean we go off-season completely and buy huge amounts of produce from the other side of the world. We grow brilliant winter vegetables in the UK and they lend themselves to hearty winter cooking. Turnips, potatoes, celeriac and cabbages are truly wonderful and just need a little bit of love and thought in order to transform them into delicious accompaniments to some of our classic dishes.

Cooking vegetables requires a gentle touch. Young, tender vegetables such as beetroot or broad beans (my favourite) require very little cooking to bring out the huge flavour hidden within. A timer is really useful in the kitchen to prevent over-cooking, and will ensure perfect results.

ASPARAGUS AND CHEESE TART WITH POACHED PHEASANT EGGS

Serves 6   *April to May*

I love unusual eggs, and one of the unsung eggs of old England is the pheasant egg. Traditionally, gamekeepers caught pheasants in February, and the birds then produced eggs for about 60 days. The pheasant eggs were incubated and brought on for the next year's birds. This is still practised by a small number of gamekeepers, but the majority of birds are brought in, in their feathered state, when either a day or a few months old.

If you can find pheasant eggs, they are wonderful. They are now appearing in quite a few restaurants. The beauty of them is that they are only available for two months of the year – I love ingredients like this and it is great to celebrate them when you can. They also coincide, almost to the day, with that most wonderfully British of ingredients, the noble asparagus.

Asparagus is fantastic, aside from having one or two notable side effects, and I don't know anyone who dislikes it. However, please don't buy it out of season, since it will have been shipped in from somewhere like Peru.

These two ingredients, combined with some tasty, strong Cheddar cheese, create a wonderful tangy tart, with the poached pheasant eggs on top providing the sauce that drips all over the egg as it is cut open. Yum!

butter, to grease the tins
500g/1lb 2oz ready-made buttery
    shortcrust pastry (pie crust)
plain (all-purpose) flour, to dust
1 egg, beaten, for egg-wash
18 spears of young asparagus, woody
    ends broken off
200g/7oz Cheddar, finely grated
250ml/9fl oz/1 generous cup double
    (heavy) cream
18 pheasant eggs (12 for the custard
    and 6 for poaching) – if you can't
    get them use quails eggs or small
    hens eggs

1 small bunch of fresh chives, finely
    chopped
1 tbsp white wine vinegar or
    cider vinegar
sea salt and freshly ground black pepper

For the salad
100g/3½oz watercress
2 tbsp olive oil
juice of ½ lemon

continues overleaf >

Use either one large quiche tin or six individual ones, all with removable bases and ideally with fluted sides. Grease the inside of the tins with a little butter. Cover and refrigerate for 30 minutes. Preheat the oven to 180°C/350°F/gas mark 4.

Roll out the pastry on a lightly floured surface to approximately 3mm/⅛ inch thick and use to line the tin(s). Line the pastry with greaseproof (wax) paper and fill with baking beans or rice. Blind bake for 15 minutes. Remove the baking beans and paper. Return the pastry case to the oven for 6–7 minutes, until the inside of the pastry case feels firm. Brush the pastry case with egg-wash, then return to the oven for a further 2 minutes.

Lightly poach the asparagus in salted water for 2 minutes, then remove and cool in iced water. Drain and dry on kitchen paper (paper towels).

Put three-quarters of the cheese, the cream and 12 of the eggs into a bowl with the chives and salt and pepper to taste and beat to combine.

Lay the asparagus spears lengthways in the pastry case (opposing end to opposing end). Fill with the cheesy custard, sprinkle a little more cheese over the top (reserving some for later), then bake in the oven at for 10–15 minutes, until the tart is just set. Remove and allow to cool a little.

Fill a shallow pan with water to a depth of about 4cm/1½ inches. Add the vinegar and bring up to just below boiling point. Lightly oil a ladle and crack a pheasant egg into it (pheasant eggs have very tough membranes, so I find it is best to cut the outside of the egg gently with a knife). Carefully roll the egg into the hot water, turning it over on to itself as you do so – this will create a perfect poached egg. Cook two or three at a time. Pheasant eggs take about 3 minutes. Once cooked, you should be able to push the top of the egg and feel that it is still runny inside. Remove the eggs as soon as they are done and gently place them in iced water. This will stop the cooking process immediately and leave the egg runny in the middle. Cook all the remaining eggs like this.

Cut the large tart into six rectangular slices, or unmould the individual tarts. Place on plates.

For the salad, put the watercress in a bowl. Combine the oil and lemon juice in a jug, then pour it over the watercress and mix. Sprinkle a few leaves around the edge of each portion of tart. Roll a poached egg onto the top of each tart. Sprinkle with the remaining grated cheese and serve.

CREAMED SPINACH WITH PARMESAN

Serves 6   *June to October*

This is the most decadent, unhealthy and utterly moreish side dish you can lay your hands on. It's fabulous with a perfectly cooked fillet steak. The spinach is a brilliant vehicle for the garlic, cream and Parmesan, and when cooked for long enough, the combination of flavours is almost religious in its intensity.

The secret to making really good creamed spinach is to use top-quality frozen spinach, from which you have wrung as much water as possible. If you have a glut of spinach in your garden you can blanch it, cool it quickly and shred it into freezer bags, then freeze. Do not use cheap Parmesan for this recipe; it really makes a difference if you buy good aged Parmesan and grate it at the last minute.

500g/1lb 2oz frozen spinach, thawed
75g/3oz/scant ½ cup butter
1 onion, peeled and thinly sliced
4 cloves of garlic, peeled and finely chopped
75ml/3fl oz/⅓ cup dry white wine
450ml/15fl oz/scant 2 cups double (heavy) cream
200g/7oz Parmesan
sea salt and freshly ground black pepper

Chop the spinach fairly finely, then put it into a clean tea towel and wring as much liquid out as you possibly can.

Heat the butter in a large shallow pan over a medium heat. Add the onion and garlic and sweat them for 10 minutes. Add the spinach and cook for a further 15 minutes. Pour in the wine and cook for 2 minutes, then add the cream. Turn the heat down to very low and cook for 1 hour, uncovered, stirring every few minutes. Once most of the cream has evaporated and the spinach looks rich and thick, it is ready.

Grate the Parmesan and stir it into the spinach, then season with salt and pepper and taste (you will probably taste several times as it is disgustingly moreish).

WATERCRESS, SPINACH AND WILD GARLIC SOUP

Serves 6   *April and May*

While I have a reputation for being something of a rabid carnivore, I am fascinated by the profusion of wild plants that can be sustainably harvested from our fields and woods at certain times of the year. Particular favourites are watercress (I live next to a stream that is teeming with the stuff from Spring through to Summer) and wild garlic. It is one of the great treats of my year to be stalking through a deciduous wood after roe deer or muntjac in late March or early April, and to smell the first hints of garlic in the air.

Traditionally known as ramsons, the leaves of this plant, especially when young, are delicious in soups or mashed into potatoes, and have myriad culinary uses. Spinach is, of course, almost miraculously good for you. It grows in huge quantities throughout the Spring and Summer in the Pot Kiln garden. All three ingredients together create a fabulous concoction.

200g/7oz watercress
200g/7oz young spinach
a large double handful of wild
    garlic leaves
200g/7oz/1 cup table salt
50g/2oz/¼ cup butter

1 white onion, peeled and roughly
    chopped
2 large baking potatoes, peeled and
    roughly chopped
sea salt and freshly ground black pepper

Pick the leaves from the watercress and discard the tough stems. Do the same to the spinach. Mix all three types of leaf together and immerse in a large sink full of cold water. Pour in the salt and mix well. Leave the leaves in the salted water for 30 minutes to kill any bugs. Drain and rinse thoroughly under fresh running water.

Place a large heavy pan on a medium heat and melt the butter. Add the onion and soften for 5 minutes. Add the potatoes and cover with 2 litres/3½ pints/8½ cups of water. Bring the water to the boil and simmer for 10-15 minutes, until the potatoes are soft. Add the spinach, watercress and wild garlic and simmer for 10–15 minutes.

Carefully transfer the hot soup to a blender and blitz furiously until a glorious vivid green, fragrant liquid appears. Return to the pan and season liberally with salt and pepper. This is a pungent, vibrant soup busting with health and vitamins.

WILD GARLIC RISOTTO

Serves 4   *Mid-March to early May*

It is a matter of some astonishment to our Continental cousins that we don't make more use of the edible plants and mushrooms that grow annually in our woods and fields. I have this on the impeccable authority of Raul van den Broeck, a Belgian über-forager with whom I had the huge pleasure of filming in his adopted home in the Forest of Dean this year for *Countrywise*. Raul has been foraging in our woods for 40-odd years and knows them intimately. On the late Spring day when I joined him, we picked masses of heady-scented wild garlic, wild hop shoots from the hedgerows, and sundry other edibles that teamed wherever we looked. The Forest of Dean is one of Britain's oldest royal hunting forests and comprises thousands of acres of ancient woodland. Due to its protected status, it (and other areas of Britain like it) is particularly rich in wild, gatherable food. If you decide to forage for your ingredients, then certain rules must be followed, namely:

1 Always ask for the permission of the landowner – most landowners are more than happy if they are politely asked and assured you are not going to ravage their land.
2 You must know what you are doing. The first few times you go out, go with an expert and make sure you have a good foraging book. Roger Phillips' *Wild Food* is considered to be the bible.
3 Never pick too much; make sure your impact on any area you are foraging is minimal.

Wild garlic is at its best when young, but even when it starts to flower, all you have to do is push the large leaves aside and pick the fresh young leaves growing underneath.

1 litre/1³⁄₄ pints/4¹⁄₄ cups vegetable stock
150g/5oz/³⁄₄ cup butter
200g/7oz/1 cup risotto rice
2 large shallots, peeled and finely chopped
125ml/4fl oz/¹⁄₂ cup dry white wine
2 handfuls of wild garlic leaves, with
  the flowers to decorate
200g/7oz Parmesan, finely grated
sea salt and freshly ground black pepper

continues overleaf >

Bring your stock up to simmering point in a large saucepan and keep it at this point.

Melt one-third of the butter in a large, heavy, not-too-deep pan over a low-medium heat. Add the rice and stir, coating every grain with melted butter. Add the shallots and cook, stirring, for 2 minutes. Add the wine. When the wine has nearly disappeared and the rice is starting to swell, add the first ladleful of hot stock. Gently stir in the stock and allow the risotto to cook for 2–3 minutes. Continue adding the stock and stirring in this way for about 17 minutes (it is very important that you don't add too much stock at any one time, or you will drown the risotto). The way to test whether it is time to add more stock is to sweep the spoon across the risotto – if the bottom of the pan stays clear of liquid for a few seconds, it is time to add more.

Cut the rest of the butter up into small pieces.

When the rice is just starting to soften (*al dente*), add the wild garlic, then the pieces of butter. Stir until the butter is incorporated, then add the Parmesan and stir well. Season to taste with salt and pepper and serve decorated with a sprinkling of wild garlic flowers.

CHILLED SUMMER COURGETTE SOUP

Serves 6   *June to October*

I am always amazed at the prolific nature of the courgette plant. I have a raised bed, about 5 x 3 metres/15 x 9ft, that is given over solely to courgettes. Once they get into full swing in mid-Summer, even a busy restaurant is hard-pressed to use the sheer number of vegetables that are produced. This soup really brings out the best in the courgette, being a fabulous colour and having a very clean flavour. It could, of course, be eaten hot, but serving it chilled accentuates the flavour. There is a significant amount of olive oil – this is an integral part of the soup and is not just there to fry the courgettes, so be bold and use the full amount.

175ml/6fl oz/scant 1 cup of olive oil
2 cloves of garlic, peeled and sliced wafer-thin
6–8 medium courgettes (zucchini), cleaned and sliced
800ml/1 pint 7fl oz/3½ cups boiling water
1 small bunch of basil
sea salt and freshly ground black pepper

Bring the oil up to a fairly high heat in a large saucepan. Add the garlic and courgettes, turn the heat down to medium and put the lid on. Stir every couple of minutes, until the courgettes are just beginning to break down.

Remove from the heat and pour in the boiling water and basil leaves. Immediately blitz with a hand blender until very fine. Season with salt and pepper and chill, covered, straight away. (The quickest way to do this is to pour the soup into a shallow, flat container, put the lid on and pop it into a freezer. This amount of soup will not affect the freezer, but the freezer will chill the soup quickly and it will retain the green colour.)

Serve in glasses on its own, or as an accompaniment to a simple starter.

PEA AND BROAD BEAN MASH

Serves 4 *June-August*

My garden is a constant joy, unless the muntjac have been to visit, in which case it can be a nightmare. This year it has been free of them, thank God, and as a result we have had a serious glut of peas and broad beans. We use them for lots of things, but this little recipe is a delight as an accompaniment to grilled fish or vegetables – the purée is vivid and fresh, both in flavour and colour. It is also delicious as an accompaniment to pâté or a terrine.

200g/7oz/1¼ cups peas, podded weight
200g/7oz/1¼ cups young or shelled
    broad (fava) beans, podded weight
sea salt
50ml/2fl oz/¼ cup olive oil
12 mint leaves
lemon juice, to taste
1 tsp freshly ground black pepper
sea salt

Cook the peas and beans in lightly salted boiling water for 3–4 minutes. Remove, drain and drop into a bowl of iced water (this will stop the cooking process and keep the vivid colour). Drain well.

Put the chilled peas and beans into a food processor and pour in the olive oil. Add the mint and a squeeze of lemon, then add the pepper and 1 tsp sea salt. Whizz until smooth, or less so if you prefer a chunky texture.

GARLICKY FRIED POTATOES

Serves 6   *Summer*

This is one of life's guilty pleasures! Use really good new potatoes and boil them until they are just tender. Use huge amounts of garlic, and way more sea salt than is good for you!

750g/1lb 11oz new potatoes, ideally Jersey Royals,
    but Charlottes are a good substitute, peeled
50ml/2fl oz/scant ¼ cup olive oil
12 cloves of garlic, peeled and squashed
3 sprigs of rosemary
1 tbsp sea salt
freshly ground black pepper

Boil the spuds in lightly salted water until they are just cooked. Drain them and dunk them in iced water or run them under a cold tap; this stops them cooking any further. Leave them to cool, then dry them and slice them in half lengthways.

Heat the olive oil in a heavy frying pan over a medium heat. Add the potatoes, garlic and rosemary and fry for 20 minutes, turning from time to time, until crisp and crunchy. Drain on kitchen paper (paper towels), then sprinkle with sea salt and black pepper and serve.

LINGUINE WITH MARSH SAMPHIRE AND LEMON OLIVE OIL

Serves 4   *June/September*

Samphire is one of our crowning-glory ingredients – growing wild around our coasts, its flavour is amazing. Not for nothing is it known as 'sea asparagus'. This recipe mixes it with pasta, which may seem a bit funny, but it works. The great thing about this dish is how few ingredients are in it – this allows the samphire to shine.

Two of my good chums, Joe and Cousin Ed, live on the north Norfolk coast and spend far more time than is responsible out and about catching things on their crab boat. I was lucky enough to have a couple of days there last summer and my abiding memory was swimming among semi-submerged fields of samphire. I paddled around gorging like a pallid manatee until dragged back into the boat on the changing tide.

Samphire is available online and in fishmongers. Buy some, even if you just boil it for 5 minutes, and eat it with melting butter and pepper.

200g/7oz linguine
100ml/3½fl oz/scant ½ cup extra-virgin olive oil
2 cloves of garlic, peeled and grated
1 unwaxed lemon
1 bunch of flat-leaf parsley, finely chopped
200g/7oz green tender marsh samphire tips
sea salt and freshly ground black pepper

Cook the linguine in lightly salted water according to the packet instructions.

Meanwhile, pour the oil into a shallow pan and set it over a medium heat. Add the garlic and let it infuse but not colour. Grate the zest of the lemon into the oil and add the juice. Add the parsley just before the pasta is cooked.

Add the samphire to the cooking pasta 2 minutes before it is done.

Drain the pasta and pour the herby lemony oil over it. Mix well, check the seasoning, and serve with cold Chablis.

CAULIFLOWER CROQUETTES

Makes 12 large croquettes   *December to April*

If there is one underrated vegetable in Britain, it is surely the cauliflower. We generally use it for only one dish, the ubiquitous cauliflower cheese, and could there be any more delicious combination than firm cauliflower florets liberally slathered in rich béchamel sauce, then baked or grilled to golden perfection?

This recipe is a neat and easy way of bringing cauliflower cheese into the 21st century. These croquettes are awesome with aioli and make a brilliant canapé when small. The key to making them is a thick béchamel sauce and a strong Cheddar. Also, we must not cook the cauliflower too long (one of our other great English traits, cooking the life out of our vegetables).

For the croquettes
600g/1lb 5oz cauliflower florets
200g/7oz mature Cheddar, grated
1 tbsp Dijon mustard
¾ tsp ground mace
¼ bunch of chives, finely chopped
2 eggs
100g/3½oz/scant ⅔ cup plain
    (all-purpose) flour
200g/7oz/1⅔ cup breadcrumbs
    (ideally Panko, see page 46)
vegetable oil, for deep-frying
sea salt and freshly ground black pepper

For the béchamel (this makes extra,
see note in method)
150g/5oz/10 tbsp butter
100g/3½oz/⅔ cup plain
    (all-purpose) flour
500ml/17fl oz/generous 2 cups
    full-fat (whole) milk
1 bay leaf
1 shallot, peeled
1 clove

For the béchamel sauce, melt the butter in a heavy pan over a low heat and add the flour. Cook gently for 5 minutes, stirring. Add the milk, a little at a time, stirring continuously, until it has all been added and the liquid is lump-free. Attach the bay leaf to the shallot using the clove as a nail. Add the shallot to the sauce and cook for 20 minutes, stirring gently the whole time, until the béchamel has thickened. Remove the shallot.

Meanwhile, cook the cauliflower florets in a pan of lightly salted boiling water until just tender, then drain, place in kitchen paper (paper towel) and wring out the water. Chop the cauliflower and mix with 300g/11oz béchamel (we have made plenty of béchamel so you have spare, which can be kept in the freezer or fridge). Add the cheese, mustard, mace and chives and season with salt and pepper to taste. Stir well.

Lay out two sheets of clingfilm (plastic wrap) on a work surface and spoon the nearly cooled filling down the centre of each. Roll up into a pressurised 'sausage', twizzling each end to ensure you have a tight seal. Place these into the fridge to set.

continues overleaf >

Beat the eggs and pour into a shallow bowl. Lay out the flour and breadcrumbs separately in their own shallow bowls. Remove the clingfilm and cut the sausage into finger-sized lengths. Heat the oil in a deep-fryer or large pan. When it is hot enough, roll the sausages in the flour, then in egg and then in breadcrumbs. Deep-fry for 3 minutes, until golden brown. Serve hot with aioli (see page 88).

TOMATO SAUCE

Makes 1 litre *June to September*

It is amazing how many uses there are for a tip-top tomato sauce. This is a far cry from the jars of sauces that are so prolific in our shops. It is easily made with supermarket ingredients and serves a multitude of purposes. While I make it with bacon, you can of course leave this out if you wish it to be vegetarian. This sauce is spectacular as a topping for a crisp pizza or simply mixed with homemade pasta and mountains of fresh Parmesan.

100ml/3½fl oz/scant ½ cup extra-virgin olive oil
4 cloves of garlic, peeled and finely chopped
4 shallots, peeled and finely chopped
50g/2oz smoked bacon lardons, very finely chopped
4 salted anchovies, finely chopped (optional)

1 tbsp baby capers
1 medium-hot red chilli (chile), finely chopped
125ml/4fl oz/½ cup dry white wine
1kg/2¼lb extremely ripe plum tomatoes, or 1kg/2¼lb Italian chopped plum tomatoes in a can
1 sprig of rosemary
sea salt and freshly ground black pepper

Pour half the oil into the bottom of a large heavy casserole and place it over a medium-low heat. Add the garlic and shallots and sweat them in the oil for 5 minutes. Add the bacon, the anchovies if using, and capers and cook for 5 minutes more. Add the chilli, then pour in the wine.

Put the tomatoes into a food processor and blitz until fine. Pour them into the pan and add the rosemary. Bring up to simmer and cook for 1 hour, uncovered, or until the sauce has reduced by a third. If you feel it needs to be richer, then pour in the remaining olive oil. Season well with salt and pepper. Remove the rosemary.

Pour the sauce hot, straight from the pan, into sterilized Kilner jars (see page 228). It will keep well in the fridge. However, I prefer to let it cool, pour it into small freezer bags and freeze, so it is always available when I need it.

RATATOUILLE ON TOAST

Serves 6   *June to September*

Ratatouille is generally a huge disappointment. When I think of it, I have a picture of the ripest vegetables glistening with glorious olive oil, slow-cooked and all held together with the most delicious tomatoes – an explosion of Summer flavours. So often it is a grotesque disappointment when it turns out to be a bunch of vegetables stewed in tomato juice.

Well, not this one! This is a real Summer staple of mine, best made in large quantities and improving day by day if kept in the fridge for 2–3 days. Served piled up on garlicky toast, there is no better Summer lunch. The important thing is to cook all the ingredients individually, then combine them. It's a job of work, but absolutely worthwhile.

4 red (bell) peppers
4 medium courgettes (zucchini)
3 red onions, peeled
3 medium aubergines (eggplant)
really good extra-virgin olive oil
12 cloves of garlic, unpeeled
600g/1lb 5oz ripe cherry tomatoes

1 x 400g can chopped Italian
    plum tomatoes
125ml/4fl oz/½ cup dry white wine
6 slices of white or brown farmhouse
    bread
a handful of basil leaves
sea salt and freshly ground black pepper

Deseed the peppers and cut them into 4cm/1½-inch chunks. Cut the courgettes into 1cm/½-inch rounds. Cut the onions into eighths and the aubergines into 2.5cm/1-inch cubes.

Heat your largest pan over a medium heat. Pour in several tablespoons of oil and brown the aubergines; they will take a little while as they soak up a lot of oil. Once done, remove from the pan. Pour in a little more oil and cook the peppers until they are softened. Remove them when done. Pour in a little more oil and cook the courgettes until they start to brown. Remove them from the pan. Now, add the onions and all but one of the garlic cloves and cook for 15 minutes or so, until they soften. Add all the tomatoes, pour in the wine and cook for 10 minutes.

Put all the vegetables back in and stir well. Reduce the heat to very low, put a lid on the pan and cook for 1 hour. Take the lid off to allow some evaporation and cook for a further 1½ hours. At the end of this time you should have a glorious, oily concoction that smells to die for. Season to taste and it's ready to eat (although it is much better the next day).

To serve, rub the bread with olive oil and the remaining garlic and toast (or barbecue) until golden. Chop the basil leaves, mix them through the hot ratatouille at the last possible minute, and pile it on top of the toast in glorious technicolour mounds.

BEETROOT ROASTED WITH PEARS AND HONEY

Serves 4 *July to October*

This recipe may sound a little bizarre, but the flavours balance astonishingly well, and the colours are vibrant. It is also extremely healthy. I grow a lot of beetroot and I particularly like some of the heritage varieties. They are really easy to grow in a garden, minding their own business until ready. I like to pick them while they are relatively small, then simply roast them after a quick scrub. This little recipe makes an outstanding accompaniment to roast pork and crackling.

8 smallish beetroot (beets), washed
    and peeled
4 ripe pears (not overripe; they need
    to be reasonably firm)
2 tbsp light olive oil
2 tbsp balsamic vinegar
2 tbsp honey
2 sprigs of rosemary, leaves picked
sea salt and freshly ground black pepper

Preheat the oven to 200°C/400°F/gas mark 6. Cut the beetroot into halves or quarters, depending on how big they are. Peel the pears and cut them into similar-sized wedges to the beetroot. Heat the oil in a heavy oven-proof pan over a medium heat and cook the beetroot for 10 minutes. Add the pears, then the balsamic and honey. Toss well. Add the rosemary and transfer the pan to the oven for 15 minutes. Remove from the oven, season with salt and pepper and serve.

CELERIAC AND WILD GARLIC SOUP

Serves 6   *May and June*

Wild garlic (otherwise known as ramsons) is one of our springtime treats.
It is hugely exciting to walk through a piece of woodland in late March
or early April (depending on the weather) and smell the first heady waft
of garlic. The young shoots are fantastic in soups. If you cannot get wild
garlic, substitute with watercress.

Celeriac is another once-underused and yet now hugely fashionable
ingredient. This ugly, head-shaped vegetable tastes utterly delicious.
It is sweet and soft in texture and, when paired with wild garlic, makes
for a clean, fresh and flavoursome dish.

50g/2oz/¼ cup butter
3 large shallots or 1 onion, peeled
    and sliced
1 large celeriac (celery root), peeled and
    cubed
1 litre/1¾ pints/4¼ cups
    vegetable stock

200ml/7fl oz/scant 1 cup double
    (heavy) cream
a large double handful of wild garlic or
    watercress, chopped
sea salt and freshly ground black pepper

Melt the butter in a heavy pan. Add the shallots or onion and sweat in the foaming
butter for 10 minutes on a medium heat. Add the celeriac and cook for a further
5 minutes.

Pour in the stock, bring to a simmer and cook until the celeriac is soft. Add the cream
and bring the soup to a simmering point, then add the wild garlic or watercress.

Immediately blitz, ladle by ladle, in a food processor (or use a hand blender). Process
until the soup is very fine in texture, and season with plenty of salt and pepper.

CELERIAC, CARROT AND CHICORY REMOULADE

Serves 4   *Summer*

A remoulade is simply a French style of coleslaw, traditionally made with raw celeriac finely cut into strips and mixed with mustard and lemon juice. As an accompaniment to cold summer dishes it is delicious, and this variation merely ups the ante somewhat. Best made a couple of hours before it is eaten to allow the flavours to mingle, this is really good served with grilled lamb chops from the barbecue and perfect with spatchcocked (butterflied) chicken (see page 88).

1 celeriac (celery root), peeled
2 carrots, peeled
1 small bunch of chives, finely chopped
2 bulbs of chicory

4 tbsp mayonnaise
1 tbsp wholegrain mustard
juice and zest of 1 unwaxed lemon
sea salt and freshly ground black pepper

This recipe is mainly an exercise in knife skills. There is no machine that can substitute for a good sharp chef's knife, although you can julienne celeriac and carrot on a mandolin, if you wish.

Slice the celeriac very thinly, then cut the slices into the finest and most even julienne you can and put into a large bowl. The better you get with a knife, the quicker it will be. Do the same with the carrots (I find the best way to cut a carrot is to cut all four sides off it, creating a square, then cut the square into slices and then into fine julienne). Add the chives.

Remove the outer leaves from the chicory and discard. Stack up the inner leaves and slice into thin ribbons.

Mix all the vegetables together. Add the mayonnaise, mustard and lemon juice and zest, mix well and season.

PUDDINGS

PUDDINGS

The pudding is a crucial part of any good meal. It should be a glorious,
naughty finish to a wonderful lunch or dinner, but it should also be able to
stand alone. As with most food, I believe that a good pudding should be very
simple. We are not all trained pastry chefs, nor do we have time to spend hours
coming up with psychedelic creations that would grace a three-star restaurant.

Apart from chocolate (which is a necessity in life), I try to use seasonal fruits
and ingredients wherever I can. I don't take this to extremes, though, because
many puddings require some exotic ingredients that cannot grow in this
country. Examples are spices – ginger, mace and nutmeg – and, of course,
fat, juicy vanilla pods (use the best and most expensive pods you can find,
since they taste out of this world). Feel free to change ingredients around.
Spices are personal things and some are more to one person's taste than
another, so if you want to change the basic flavour of things, then go ahead.

Precision is much more important in baking than it is in most of my recipes.
If you do not weigh out ingredients, your baking will not perform as
described, so invest in a good set of scales to keep things on track.

If there are only two puddings that you cook from this book, then firstly make
My mother Gillian's chocolate brandy cake (see page 210) – it is seriously
easy, does not need cooking and will blow any dedicated chocoholic's mind.
Eat sparingly, however, for it redefines rich. Secondly, please bake the Sticky
stem ginger and walnut cake (see page 209). I wanted to create a cake that
reminded me of the ginger cakes I used to have as a kid, and so played
around with this recipe for ages. Make sure that when you pull the cake out
of the oven you pour all that gorgeous stem-ginger syrup over it when it is
hot. The syrup soaks in and gives the most moreish pudding ever. It's like
sticky toffee pudding taken to the next level.

Have fun and don't worry about the calories!

SCOTCH PANCAKES WITH HONEY CREAM

Serves 8   *All year round*

These simple little pancakes (also known as drop scones) have been a firm favourite of mine for as long as I can remember. The great thing about them is that, once made, they can be eaten straight away, or you can stick them in Tupperware and eat them over a week. My favoured way to devour them is slathered with butter, then covered in Marmite (yeast extract), which is a lot better than it sounds!

I cooked these for a *Countrywise Kitchen* shoot in north Yorkshire. We were filming a story about honey with a lovely beekeeper called Alan, who had a real affinity with his little charges. I had to get into a bee suit and extract a honeycomb, which cheesed off the bees no end. I also had to control my fear physically for the first time in years, as literally thousands of bees dive-bombed my bee suit. It held up, so no stings for me, unlike the poor soundman, whose hands were uncovered and got mullered.

The honey was amazing, and the combination of the raspberries (from their pick your own), the pancakes and the clotted cream really worked a treat. This makes for a great afternoon tea indulgence.

250g/9oz/1⅔ cups self-raising (self-rising) flour
125g/4oz/generous ½ cup caster (superfine) sugar
2 eggs, well beaten
125ml/4fl oz/½ cup milk
vegetable oil

1 tbsp super-duper honey, plus extra to serve
150g/5oz clotted cream
200g/7oz raspberries
1 sprig of mint, shredded
a pinch of salt

Mix the flour, sugar and salt in a bowl. Add the beaten eggs and mix well. Add the milk and beat with a whisk until no lumps remain. The consistency should be thick and clinging.

Heat a non-stick pan to a medium heat (if you do this with a camping stove, be careful not to melt the tailgate of your pickup truck as I did). Using a piece of kitchen paper (paper towel), wipe a little oil over the surface of the pan. Pour a ladleful of batter into the pan, tilt it to coat the bottom evenly and cook until bubbles appear. Flip the pancake and cook for 2 more minutes, then remove it from the pan and keep warm. Keep going with the rest of the mixture until you have made a stack of pancakes, oiling the pan as necessary between each one.

Mix the honey with the cream. Sprinkle the pancakes with raspberries and drizzle with more honey. Pour a dollop of cream over the top and sprinkle with shredded mint.

RHUBARB RICE PUDDING

Serves 6   *February to May*

Rhubarb is quintessentially British – and the first fruit (well, it's actually a veg!) of the year, which to my mind makes it properly special. It works well in a rice pudding, which I find can be very sweet. The acidity of the rhubarb just works, and that's all there is to it.

I like to use old-fashioned pudding rice, but if you have any problems finding it, then by all means use risotto rice; after all, what we want is a short-grained rice with a high starch content.

Rice puddings fall into two categories. First, there is the one that my dad used to make me when I was a kid – baked in the oven with lots of nutmeg, a runny texture, and a golden skin. The other type is cooked more like a risotto, but with lots of double cream and vanilla. The consistency of this one will be more like a runny risotto, and it is really easy to do.

100g/3½oz/½ cup butter
200g/7oz/1 cup pudding rice
600ml/1 pint/2½ cups double (heavy) cream
250g/9oz/1¼ cups caster (superfine) sugar
2 vanilla pods (beans)
500g/1lb 2oz rhubarb, trimmed

Melt the butter in a big shallow pan over a medium-low heat, then add the rice, stirring well to ensure all the grains are coated. After 5 minutes, add a third of the cream and half the sugar and bring it up to heat gently. Split and scrape one of the vanilla pods and add it to the pan. Cook for about 15 minutes, adding more cream from time to time and stirring, until the rice is *al dente* and the cream is used up.

Meanwhile, cut the rhubarb into 5cm/2-inch chunks and pop it in a separate pan, together with the other vanilla pod and the rest of the sugar. Add no water, but cook it over a low heat, stirring from time to time, for 15 minutes until it forms a delicious compote. Taste it to see if it needs more sugar.

Serve the rice pudding hot with rhubarb compote on top. Perfect with a good pudding wine.

SUMMER PUDDING AND SLOE-GIN ROLL

Serves 6   *Late Summer/Autumn*

I love making this pudding later on in the Summer because I inevitably have
a huge amount of frozen berries and red fruits squirreled away in the freezer.
Fruits that have been frozen seem to work particularly well for this Summer
pudding; they certainly take on the alcohol well, perhaps because by freezing
the fruit we are breaking down its cell structure.

Sloe gin, or any fruit gin, transforms this English Summer staple into
an X-rated dessert. I make masses of sloe gin and damson gin in the late
Autumn every year, and it is just about perfect by the following Summer.

The Berkshire hedgerows abound with wild plums, damsons and sloes from
mid-Summer right through to late Autumn. The trick is to pick the plums
and sloes as they ripen, then open-freeze them on trays and transfer them
to freezer bags once they are hard – this prevents the fruit from clumping
together in a solid mass in the freezer.

4 tbsp runny honey
1kg/2¼lb mixed berries
   (I like a mixture of redcurrants,
   blackcurrants, blackberries and
   raspberries), plus extra fruit to serve

6 tbsp sloe gin
6 medium-thick slices of white bread
   (which should be slightly stale)
clotted or double (heavy) cream, to serve

Mix 75ml/2½fl oz/¼ cup water with the honey in a large saucepan and turn the
heat to high. Once the honey has dissolved, bring the mixture to the boil and add the
fruit. Turn the heat down and stir for a couple of minutes. Pour the fruit and juice
through a sieve into a bowl and put the fruit to one side. Mix the sloe gin into the
fruit juice.

Clear your largest work surface and cover an area 60cm/24 inches long by 45cm/
18 inches wide with several layers of clingfilm (plastic wrap). Cut the crusts from
the bread and soak each slice in the juice. Lay the soaked slices on the clingfilm,
overlapping slightly. Spoon the berries down the centre of the bread evenly, making
sure all the remaining juice is poured on the fruit and bread.

Now, using the clingfilm to help you, roll the bread into a log, then roll up the
clingfilm and twizzle the ends to create a tight, pressurized 'sausage'. Place in the
fridge for 12 hours.

To serve, unroll the clingfilm carefully, or remove it with scissors, lay the log on to
a serving dish and surround with extra fruit. Cut the log into big slices and devour
with clotted or double (heavy) cream.

GOOSEBERRY FOOL
WITH HOMEMADE SHORTBREAD

Makes 6 fools (shortbread makes a biscuit tin full)   *Late Spring/early Summer*

This recipe does not have to be made with gooseberries; indeed this is the sort of fool that can be made throughout the Summer with different ingredients as they come into season, starting perhaps with rhubarb in the spring and finishing with Autumn raspberries. But gooseberries are as English as it gets, so let's make a start there.

I think a dessert like this needs contrast, and that is where this delicious shortbread comes into play. Make a tin-full of it (you might as well), and it will keep for ages if sealed.

For the fool
300g/11oz gooseberries (or any
    other soft fruit), washed
100ml/3½fl oz/scant ½ cup
    runny honey
50ml/2¼fl oz/¼ cup water
500ml/17fl oz/2 generous cups
    whipping cream

For the shortbread
200g/7oz/scant 1 cup salted butter,
    plus extra to grease
110g/3¾oz/⅔ cup fine oatmeal
110g/3¾oz/⅔ cup wholemeal flour
125g/4oz/scant 1 cup plain
    (all-purpose) flour
3 tsp ground ginger
½ tsp baking soda
150g/5oz/¾ cup brown sugar

Place the gooseberries, honey and water together in a steel pan. (You can add more or less honey to this recipe, depending on the sweetness of your tooth – personally I think gooseberry fool should be tart.) Cook on a very low heat until the gooseberries start to break down. Allow the mixture to cool, then pass it through muslin (cheesecloth) to remove any stalky bits. Whip the cream to soft peaks, then fold it gently through the cooled gooseberry mixture. Pour into glasses and chill in the fridge for several hours.

For the shortbread, preheat the oven to 160°C/325°F/gas mark 3. Lightly grease a shallow baking tray (sheet) or loose-bottomed medium round cake tin. Place all the dry ingredients in a food processor and blitz on a high speed for 30 seconds. Fit a paddle to the food processor or move the mixture to a food mixer.

Now, melt the butter in a saucepan over a low-medium heat, then pour it into the food mixer and mix well for 2 minutes. Press the mixture down firmly on the tray or tin. Score the top where you wish the shortbread to break and bake for 45 minutes. Allow to cool on a wire rack, then break into pieces.

Serve the fool with pieces of shortbread.

SWEET CHERRY PIE

Serves 4   *June/July*

Cherries are the best – fat, ripe, sunny lumps of plumptious delight. Many is the time I have eaten a bagful, only to regret it an hour later. This is a recipe I first cooked years ago in Australia, where I briefly worked as a pastry chef.

For the pastry
300g/10oz/generous 2 cups plain
   (all-purpose) flour, plus extra to dust
2 tbsp icing (confectioner's) sugar
1 large pinch of table salt
175g/6oz/¾ cup cold unsalted
   butter, diced
4 medium egg yolks
4 tbsp ice-cold water
crème fraîche, to serve

For the filling
juice of 1 small lemon
100ml/3½fl oz/scant ½ cup Kirsch
100g/3½oz/½ cup good-quality
   cherry jam
150g/5oz/¾ cup caster (superfine) sugar
1kg/2¼lb stoned (pitted) cherries
3 tbsp arrowroot

For the pastry, sift the flour into a bowl with the icing (confectioner's) sugar and salt. Transfer to a food processor and whizz with the butter until the mixture resembles coarse breadcrumbs. Whisk together 3 egg yolks with the water and add to the processor slowly, whizzing with each addition, until the mixture resembles a soft dough. Gather up the dough to form a ball, knead briefly, divide in two, wrap in clingfilm (plastic wrap), then chill both portions in the fridge for 1 hour.

For the filling, mix the lemon juice, Kirsch and jam in a frying pan. Place it over a low heat. Add the sugar and cherries, letting the ingredients get to know each other briefly. Cool slightly before adding the arrowroot. Let the mixture stand for 25 minutes, then stir once more.

Preheat the oven to 220°C/425°F/gas mark 7. Roll out half the pastry on a lightly floured surface to line a 23cm/9-inch greased tart tin (pie dish). Roll out the second half of the pastry to form a circle to cover the tin. Put the circle on a sheet of baking parchment and chill both the dough-lined tin and the circle in the fridge until needed. Pile the cherries into the lined flan case until it becomes a gently swelling mound.

Brush the edges of the pastry crust with water, then lay the pastry lid on top. Trim the edges, then crimp together firmly. Beat the remaining egg yolk and then brush it over the top of the pastry. Cut a hole in the centre of the pie to allow steam to escape. Bake for 20 minutes, then reduce the heat to 180°C/350°F/gas mark 4 and bake for a further 30-40 minute. If the pastry is darkening too rapidly, cover loosely with tin foil. Serve the pie warm or cold, with crème fraîche.

CHERRY CLAFOUTIS

Serves 4   *Summer*

The best way to describe this foreign-sounding dessert is to think of it as a boozy Yorkshire pudding eaten as, well... a pudding! It is seriously easy to make, and quite delicious. I love cherries, and while they are at their best eaten straight off the tree, this dish makes a good alternative to the cherry pie recipe on page 202. It is devilishly quick to make and seriously wonderful to serve. I put rum in with the cherries, since booze and fruit are lifelong friends... Lastly, remember that the batter should be thin if you want a light and fluffy pudding.

25g/1oz/2 tbsp butter, plus extra to grease the pan
750g/1lb 11oz stoned (pitted) red cherries
100g/3½oz/scant ½ cup caster (superfine) sugar
seeds from 1 vanilla pod
1 small glass of rum (dark rich rum)
125g/4oz/scant 1 cup plain (all-purpose) flour
350ml/12fl oz/1½ cups milk
3 large eggs
a pinch of salt
whipped cream, to serve

Preheat the oven to 220°C/425°F/gas mark 7. Melt the butter in a heavy ovenproof pan over a medium heat. Stir in the cherries and half the sugar, then the vanilla seeds. Pour in the rum and flame. Reduce the liquid until the cherries are sticky, then reduce the heat.

Make the batter. Mix the remaining sugar and the flour in a bowl, then whisk in the milk, ensuring there are no lumps. Beat in the eggs, one at a time, and add the salt.

Brush the sides of the pan containing the cherries with melted butter. Pour in the batter until it comes to 2.5cm/1 inch from the top. Bake in the oven until cooked through and risen – about 25 minutes.

Remove from the oven and serve with lashings of whipped cream.

MARMALADE MADELEINES

Makes 2 trays of madeleines   *All year round*

Ever since my days as an apprentice in France, I have had an addiction that is nicotine-like in its voracity for these delightful little scallop-shaped French cakes. I have Anglicized these madeleines with the addition of some strong English marmalade.

It is all-important that you find the right moulds for baking your madeleines. I suggest you go to a kitchen shop or on to the internet and buy some of the siliconized rubber baking moulds. These are fabulous, as nothing will ever stick to them and they will last nearly forever.

Madeleines are the perfect afternoon tea cake and can be treated in the same way as a scone – split in half and served with double cream and English marmalade.

150g/5oz/¾ cup butter, plus extra to grease
4 medium eggs
100g/3½oz/scant ½ cup caster (superfine) sugar
350g/12oz/2⅓ cups plain (all-purpose) flour
10g/¼oz baking powder
zest of 2 oranges
1¼ tsp mixed spice
a pinch of salt
200g/7oz/1 cup strong Seville orange marmalade
juice of 1 orange

Preheat the oven to 160°C/325°F/gas mark 3. Lightly butter the madeleine moulds.

Combine the eggs, sugar, flour, baking powder, orange zest, mixed spice and salt in a mixing bowl and mix well.

Heat the butter in a pan until golden (*beurre noisette*), then turn off the heat and add the marmalade and orange juice. Once the marmalade has dissolved, add this mixture to the rest of the ingredients and mix evenly.

Spoon the mixture evenly into the madeleine moulds. Bake for 8–10 minutes until golden. Serve warm.

PEAR, GINGER AND FRANGIPANE TART

Makes a 28cm/11-inch tart *Late Summer/Autumn*

Britain is renowned for the quality of its pears. There are few fruits so delicious as a perfectly ripe, sweet and sugary pear. The key is to eat them in season – don't buy pears that have been shipped in from abroad and picked when still virtually raw, for they will be hard, relatively tasteless and deeply disappointing. My advice is to try different varieties of pear until you find one you really like. The combination with frangipane (the delicious filling for a Bakewell tart), especially when combined with a little hit of ginger, is quite irresistible.

400g/14oz shortcrust pastry (pie crust), homemade (see page 202) or ready-made, chilled
plain (all-purpose) flour, to dust
250g/9oz/1¼ cups butter, softened, plus extra for greasing
250g/9oz/1¼ cups caster (superfine) sugar
4 medium eggs, plus 1 for egg-wash (optional)

125g/4oz/generous 1 cup ground almonds
125g/4oz/generous 1 cup pulsed hazelnuts (whizzed in food processor)
3 balls of stem (preserved) ginger in syrup, drained and finely chopped
4 tbsp ginger liqueur or amaretto
4 ripe pears
clotted cream, to serve

Preheat the oven to 180°C/350°F/gas mark 4. Grease a 28cm/11-inch loose-bottomed fluted tart tin (pie dish).

Roll out the pastry on a lightly floured surface to a thickness of 3mm/⅛ inch and use it to line the tin. Prick the surface. Line the pastry with greaseproof (wax) paper and fill with baking beans or rice. Blind bake for 15 minutes. Remove the baking beans and paper. Return the pastry case to the oven for 6–7 minutes. Brush the pastry case with egg-wash and return to the oven for 2 minutes. Lower the oven temperature to 170°C/325°F/gas mark 3.

Place the butter and sugar in a bowl and beat with an electric whisk until pale and fluffy; this takes at least 5 minutes. Add the eggs, one by one, beating all the time. Turn the speed down and add the nuts. Mix gently, then add the stem ginger and liqueur. Peel the pears, cut them in half lengthways and remove the cores. Slice the pears on a diagonal and arrange them in a neat pattern within the tart case.

Pour the frangipane over the pears until it comes to just below the top of the pastry. Bake for 25 minutes, or until a knife pushed into the tart comes out clean. Halfway through the cooking process, glaze the top of the frangipane with beaten egg. Allow the tart to cool. Remove from the tin and serve with clotted cream.

STICKY STEM GINGER AND WALNUT CAKE

Makes 2 cakes   *All year round*

Stem ginger is one of those great British ingredients; it is determinedly old-fashioned and can be used for dozens of different applications, but it's best when baked into a gooey cake along the lines of this one. I have added walnuts to this recipe because the two flavours really complement each other – feel free to leave them out if they are not your cup of tea. This cake is great to bake in advance of a party because, due to its extreme gooeyness, it will keep very well.

125g/4oz/generous ½ cup cold butter, cut into small pieces, plus extra to grease
1 tbsp ground ginger
a pinch of ground cinnamon
250g/9oz/2 cups self-raising (self-rising) flour
1 tsp bicarbonate of soda (baking soda)
275ml/9½fl oz/1¼ cups milk
125g/4oz/⅓ cup black treacle (blackstrap molasses)
125g/4oz/⅓ cup maple syrup
125g/4oz/generous ½ cup muscovado (dark brown) sugar
100g/3½oz stem (preserved) ginger in syrup, drained (retain the syrup) and
    finely chopped
1 egg, beaten
100g/3½oz/1 cup chopped walnuts

Preheat the oven to 160°C/325°F/gas mark 3. Grease a 23cm x 13cm (9-inch x 5-inch) loaf tin (pan) with butter and line with greaseproof (wax) paper. Mix the spices, flour and bicarbonate of soda together in a mixing bowl. Add the butter and rub in with your hands until you have a breadcrumb texture.

Heat up the milk in a saucepan over a medium heat and add the treacle, maple syrup and sugar. Stir until the sugar has dissolved, then, stirring all the time, bring the mixture up to a simmer. Add the stem ginger. Mix the treacle mixture into the flour and add the egg. Beat well with an electric whisk until you have a thick loose mixture, then stir through the walnuts. Pour the mixture into the tin and bake for 1 hour, or until a skewer pushed into the cake comes out cleanish (if you wish the cake to be stickier in the middle, cook it for slightly less time).

Now, using a fine skewer, prick the top of the cake several dozen times and pour 5–6 tablespoonfuls of stem ginger syrup over it. When cool, cut into wedges and serve with cups of strong tea.

MY MOTHER GILLIAN'S CHOCOLATE BRANDY CAKE

Serves 10   *All year round*

One of my enduring memories of childhood is the trek from Berkshire to Lancashire, where my mother's family come from. We would make this journey two or three times a year and certain aspects of the visit were always keenly anticipated, this cake being one of them. My mother, Gillian, would have made this the day before our departure, knowing that it would be high on our list of expectations.

The cake is exceedingly rich and should be eaten only in very small amounts. As a child I remember gorging on it, as one did, and then feeling extremely sick as a result. The original recipe was studded throughout with glacé cherries, which were the one element I keenly disliked. I have therefore replaced these with pistachios, which I love, but you can stick pretty much anything you want in the mixture.

225g/8oz/1 cup butter, plus extra to grease
225g/8oz digestive biscuits (graham crackers)
225g/8oz chocolate, 70% cocoa solids, broken into pieces
2 medium eggs
85g/3¼oz/scant ½ cup caster (superfine) sugar
60g/2½oz/½ cup pistachio nuts
60g/2½/½ cup walnuts, chopped
1 small glass of brandy or dark rum

Butter a 23cm x 13cm (9-inch x 5-inch) loaf tin (pan) or mould of a similar size. Crush the biscuits coarsely and put them to one side. Carefully melt the chocolate with the butter over a very low heat. Beat the eggs and sugar together in a bowl until pale and fluffy, then beat in the melted chocolate and butter (I find an electric hand whisk is really good for this). Fold in three-quarters of the pistachios and walnuts, all the brandy or rum and the crushed digestives. Mix well and pour into the tin or mould.

Decorate the top with the remaining nuts and put the cake in the refrigerator to set. Slice very thinly and serve with afternoon tea.

EARL GREY'S BURNT CREAM

Serves 8   *All year round*

Ever since the dim and dark days of my childhood I have adored crème brûlée, and it remains in my top three puddings to this day.

I can't stand the trend of bunging red fruits in crème brûlée. In this recipe, the silky and fabulous custard is accentuated with a hint of Earl Grey tea; the scent of bergamot really complements the pudding.

The great danger with any baked custard is the cream curdling during cooking. The secret is a low temperature and turning halfway through.

200ml/7fl oz/scant 1 cup milk
325ml/11fl oz/1½ cups double (heavy) cream
2 tsp loose Earl Grey tea leaves
125g/4oz egg yolks
75g/3oz/⅓ cup caster (superfine) sugar, plus
    100g/3½oz/scant ½ cup, for brûléeing the tops

Preheat the oven to 120°C/250°F/gas mark ½. Pour the milk and cream into a large pan and bring up to scalding point – that is, when the bubbles just start to rise.

Wrap the loose tea leaves in a 15cm/6-inch square piece of muslin (cheesecloth) and immerse them in the hot cream and milk. Leave to stand for 5 minutes, then remove and discard the muslin and tea leaves. The Earl Grey will have lightly infused the cream and milk mixture.

Beat together the egg yolks and the 75g/3oz/⅓ cup sugar in a large bowl with an electric whisk, until the mixture is pale yellow and fluffy. Pour the milk and cream mixture into the egg yolks and sugar, whisking while you do so.

Pour the custard into 8 ramekins or shallow individual heatproof dishes. Place the ramekins in a deep roasting tin (pan), pour 2.5cm/1 inch of water into the tin to create a bain marie and bake for 14 minutes. Turn the tin and cook for a further 14 minutes.

Remove from the oven and leave to cool. The pots of custard will keep in the fridge for 3–4 days. To serve, sprinkle the top with the remaining sugar and caramelize with a blowtorch (you can do this under a hot grill, but make sure the ramekins are close to the element).

BLACK TREACLE TART

Serves 10   *All year round*

I have never understood why the great classic treacle tart is always presented pale in colour and made exclusively with golden syrup. Using black treacle gives the slightly bitter and less sweet flavour I think should be associated with this fantastic recipe. You can, of course, make shortcrust pastry yourself. However, shop-bought pastry is now so good that I see no fault in buying it ready-made for this pudding.

butter, to grease
400g/14oz ready-made shortcrust
    pastry (pie crust), chilled
plain (all-purpose) flour, to dust
2 egg yolks, beaten, for egg-wash
1 apple
220g/7¾oz/⅔ cup black treacle
    (blackstrap molasses), plus 1 extra tsp

4 balls of stem (preserved) ginger in
    syrup, drained and finely chopped
220g/7¾oz/⅔ cup golden (light
    corn) syrup
zest and juice of 3 unwaxed lemons
175g/6oz/1½ cups breadcrumbs
    (ideally Panko, see page 46), plus
    40g/1½oz/⅓ cup for top of the tart

Preheat the oven to 180°C/350°F/gas mark 4. Grease a 28cm/11-inch loose-bottomed fluted tart tin (pie dish).

Roll out the pastry on a lightly floured surface to a thickness of 3mm/⅛ inch and use it to line the tin. Line the pastry with greaseproof (wax) paper and fill with baking beans or rice. Blind bake for 15 minutes. Remove the baking beans and paper. Return the pastry case to the oven and bake for a further 6–7 minutes, until it is dry but not coloured. Brush the pastry case with egg-wash and return it to the oven for 2 minutes.

Peel and finely chop the apple and steam it for 5 minutes, until soft. Spread the extra teaspoon of black treacle over the bottom of the cooked pastry case and place the pieces of steamed apple evenly on top. Mix together the treacle, ginger, syrup, lemon zest and juice and breadcrumbs in a saucepan over a low heat for a few minutes. Pour into the pastry and spread evenly to fill it.

Sprinkle the extra breadcrumbs on top of the tart and gently rub them in to dry out the top layer. Bake in the oven for 12 minutes. When cooked, remove the tart from the tart tin and allow to cool on a wire rack. This delicious pudding is amazing served with vanilla or cardamom ice cream.

ECCLES CAKES

Makes 12 cakes   *Winter*

Eccles cakes are a Lancastrian speciality, a staple of post-war Britain and terribly unfashionable. They are, however, utterly delicious and completely moreish, especially when served as a pudding with slowly melting ice cream. They are also incredibly easy to make, being essentially a minced pie crossed with a pasty. We will add an alcoholic element to ours that is not essential, but is damn good.

150g/5oz/¾ cup butter
200g/7oz/1 cup dark brown sugar
200g/7oz/1⅓ cups currants, soaked
    in boiling water and drained
6 balls of stem (preserved) ginger in
    syrup, drained and finely chopped
2 tsp ground cinnamon
1 tsp freshly grated nutmeg
zest of 1 orange

zest of 1 unwaxed lemon
100g/3½oz/½ cup mixed candied peel
3 tbsp dark rum
2 tbsp ground almonds
750g/1lb 11oz puff pastry
plain (all-purpose) flour, to dust
2 eggs, beaten, for egg-wash
100g/3½oz/½ cup caster
    (superfine) sugar

Preheat the oven to 200°C/400°F/gas mark 6. Melt the butter with the brown sugar in a large pan. Remove from the heat and stir in the currants, ginger, cinnamon, nutmeg, orange and lemon zest and mixed peel. Pour in the rum and add the ground almonds. Mix well and allow to cool.

Roll out 12 discs of pastry on a lightly floured surface to approximately 5mm/¼ inch thick. Place a spoonful of the filling on one-half of each of these discs. Brush the egg-wash around the edges of the pastry. Fold the pastry over to make a parcel and gently press down to make sure you have a seal.

Lay the Eccles cakes on a piece of baking parchment on a baking tray (sheet). Using the tip of a sharp knife, cut through the top of each cake three or four times. Brush the cakes liberally with egg-wash, then sprinkle with caster sugar. Bake for 20 minutes, or until golden brown. Serve hot with vanilla ice cream.

BREAD, PRESERVES AND BASICS

BREAD, PRESERVES AND BASICS

Bread is the stuff of life. Making it is the closest thing to alchemy that I know. It is a source of endless wonder that water, flour and yeast can produce such an amazing result as a good loaf. Bread is not hard to make and there are many courses available teaching the rudiments of this ancient art. For those of you who don't mind a cop-out, you can always resort to an automatic bread machine, which still gives great results – but I would implore you to try some of the recipes in this book. They are all simple, they work, and are used daily both at my pub, the Pot Kiln, and at my cookery school. The satisfaction of making bread by hand is akin to painting a work of art (I was going to write 'a great work of art', but practice will make it perfect!).

Flour and yeast are the most important elements in breadmaking. Flour needs to be strong (bread), and can be white, wholemeal or rye. Pure wholemeal (wholewheat) flour is difficult to make a light loaf out of, so I always mix it with another flour.

Yeast can be bought in granule form (which needs activating in water), in instant form (which just gets mixed with the flour), or as fresh yeast. Simply mix the yeast with warm water (the temperature should be that of a tepid bath – generally after you have fallen asleep in it!) and a little sugar to help it along.

The most common cause of a rock-hard and heavy loaf is the use of too much flour when kneading. I find that wet doughs, ones that are quite sticky when mixed, produce by far the best results. Glaze your loaf with beaten egg and milk before you bake it to give a really good result and do not rush, for you can't hurry bread.

Preserving is surely the most old-fashioned of the culinary arts. We can barely imagine a time before refrigeration, and yet this was what everyone had to contend with a scant 100 years ago. The nature of the countryside was that of feast or famine, with Winter being a time of hardship and belt-tightening. Thus folk had to preserve nature's bounty in any way they could.

There are really five ways in which we can preserve food, and all fight the growth of harmful bacteria and decay in different ways. They are:

Drying: this preserves food by removing the bacterial habitat and has the advantage of reducing weight. Great examples are dried fish and biltong (dried meat), which lasts for years and is easily rehydrated by chewing.

Salting: salt is one of nature's deadliest poisons – just ask your doctor. It bursts the cells, draws out moisture and prevents bacteria growing. However, it preserves food in a similar way to drying.

Heating: this is the most common way to preserve food. Heating to a certain temperature (usually 121°C/ 250°F) kills all bacteria. If food is sealed at heat in sterile containers, it can survive in ambient temperatures for ages.

Adding sugar: sugar behaves a bit like salt, and totally sugary environments are sterile, or nearly so; 3,000-year-old honey has been found to be edible. This is why we use so much sugar when making jam – coupled with heat, of course.

Smoking: smoke and heat, or smoke and salt, combine to form very effective preservatives. While today smoke is used more for flavour, in the old days it was mainly used to keep off insects.

BREWERY BREAD WITH CRYSTAL MALT

Makes 1 loaf   *All year round*

A wise man once said, 'Bread is life.' For many of my customers at The Pot Kiln pub, beer is life also. By combining the two, I think we have something special. The beauty of real ale is that it is a living product full of natural yeasts. By making bread, using beer as both the liquid and the raising agent, you are creating something with a unique flavour. This is one of the most popular breads we make.

One of the most important ingredients in the production of real ale is malted barley. Different strengths of malted barley produce different flavoured and coloured beers, and my favourite is golden crystal malt. Dave Maggs, who owns the West Berkshire Brewery just up the road from me, uses locally produced crystal malt to make several of his beers, including the Royal Wedding Ale, which we watched him make on *Countrywise*.

I love to sprinkle that delicious, crunchy malt over this bread just before it goes into the oven. The results are fantastic.

250g/9oz/1½ cups strong wholemeal (wholewheat) flour
250g/9oz/1⅔ cups strong white (bread) flour, plus extra to dust
a handful of crystal malt
1 tbsp salt
20g/¾oz instant (active dry) yeast
30g/1¼oz/2½ tbsp butter, melted, plus extra to grease
300ml/10fl oz/1¼ cups good local beer
1 egg, for egg-wash
onion seeds
sea salt

Mix all the dry ingredients except the onion seeds and salt together in a large bowl, then make a well in the centre and pour in the melted butter and beer. Stir to form a dough.

Tip the dough out on to a lightly floured work surface and knead for 10 minutes, then put it back into the bowl and leave it to rest in a warm place for 1 hour.

Return the dough to the floured work surface and shape it into a ball, then flatten it and roll it up. Put the dough on a greased baking sheet and leave it to rise for a further hour.

Preheat the oven to 200°C/400°F/gas mark 6. Beat the egg. Cut several slashes across the top of the bread and glaze with the egg. Sprinkle liberally with onion seeds and sea salt. Bake for 30 minutes, then transfer to a wire rack to cool.

BASIC WHITE BREAD

Makes 1 loaf *All year round*

Historically, white bread was purely for the wealthy and was a status symbol, which today we take for granted. The bread that the peasants ate would have been coarse wholemeal, containing large amounts of husk and impurities. However, modern processed white bread is made with bleached white flour, so making your own from a high-quality strong white bread flour can only be a good thing. This is easy to make, does not require a bread machine, and gives the home baker a base from which to experiment.

500g/1lb 2oz/3⅓ cups strong white
   (white bread) flour, plus extra to dust
a large pinch of sea salt
15g/½oz instant (active dry) or fresh yeast

200ml/7fl oz/scant 1 cup warm water
1 medium egg
100ml/3½fl oz/scant ½ cup milk

Place the flour in a large bowl, add the salt and mix well.

If using instant yeast, pour it over the flour (if using fresh yeast, whisk it into the warm water; make sure the water is the temperature of a tepid bath, if it is any hotter you will kill the yeast). Make a well in the middle of the flour and, using a wooden spoon, add the warm (see above) water (or warm water and fresh yeast), mixing until you have a slightly soggy-looking paste. Tip this paste onto a well-floured surface, then knead for 10–15 minutes, adding flour if necessary, until the dough becomes firm and elastic and ceases to stick to the work surface.

Put the dough into a floured mixing bowl, cover with a clean damp cloth and put it in a warm place such as an airing cupboard for 1 hour.

Remove the dough from the mixing bowl and place it on a floured work surface. Form it into a sausage shape and put it into a non-stick baking tin (pan). The dough should come two-thirds of the way up the inside of the tin.

Beat the egg and milk together, then paint the top of the dough with this egg-wash. Allow to rise for 30–40 minutes, until the dough comes above the top of the baking tin (pan).

Preheat the oven to 220°C/425°F/gas mark 7. Brush the top of the dough again lightly with the egg-wash and bake on a baking tray (sheet) for 10 minutes, then turn the oven down to 180°C/350°F/gas mark 4 and bake for a further 20 minutes. Tip the bread out and check that the sides and bottom of the loaf are fully baked. Cool on a wire rack for 1 hour before cutting.

MOROCCAN FLATBREAD

Makes 12 flatbreads   *All year round*

Flatbreads are an essential part of life in North Africa and the Middle East. They are very simple to prepare and really lend themselves to outdoor or barbecue cooking. I love to make them quite spicy, adding turmeric, cumin and often fresh chilli (chile) and coriander (cilantro).

375g/13oz/2½ cups plain (all-purpose) flour, plus extra to dust
2 tsp instant (active dry) yeast
1 tsp salt
1 tsp turmeric
1 tsp ground cumin
1 tbsp finely chopped mint or coriander (cilantro)
225ml/8fl oz/1 cup warm water
olive oil

Place all the dry ingredients including the herbs in a large mixing bowl, stirring them well. Make a well in the middle of the flour and, using a wooden spoon, add the lukewarm water, mixing until you have a slightly sticky dough with no visible flour left (we are not after a traditional firm bread dough).

Place the dough on a liberally floured work surface. Sprinkle more flour over the top, then knead until the dough is pliable, soft and even.

Pour a generous glug of oil into the mixing bowl and plonk the dough in it. Make sure all the dough is covered in oil. Cover with a clean damp cloth and put in a warm place such as an airing cupboard for 1 hour. The dough will double or more in size.

To cook the flatbread, remove a 5-cm/2-inch diameter ball (it depends how large you want your flatbread to be) and place on a well-oiled surface. With the heel of your hand, flatten the dough ball into a disc roughly 20cm/8 inches in diameter.

Once you have half a dozen discs of dough ready, preheat a non-stick or cast-iron pan on a medium-hot heat, brush the pan lightly with olive oil and cook each flatbread for 2 minutes on either side (longer if you are doing a larger bread). While the first side cooks, take a peek underneath, lifting one side of the bread with a flat spatula to see how it's doing. If your bread burns underneath while it's still very opaque on top, this means your heat is too high, so lower it a notch. If your bread is still white (not browning) underneath and all the surface becomes translucent, this means your heat is too low, so bring it up a notch.

The flatbread will bubble and rise and, when cooked, will have a beautiful spongy texture that soaks up juices from kebabs and roasted meats better than any normal bread could hope to do. This bread was designed to be eaten with the marinated beef skewers on page 26.

FOCACCIA

Makes 1 large focaccia   *All year round*

Focaccia is one of the first breads that I ever taught myself to make. This recipe was perfected over years of practice and produces the ultimate light, spongy, olive oil-infused loaf.

When cooked in our wood-fired oven at The Pot Kiln, it is positively joyous, and so versatile. What is great about this bread from a beginner's point of view is that it is virtually foolproof, always rises and the result from your guests' perspective, is very impressive. The other big benefit of focaccia is that, due to its high oil content, it keeps fantastically.

15g/good ½oz of instant (active dry) yeast
1 tbsp sea salt, plus extra for the dough
750g/1lb 11oz/5 cups strong white
   (white bread) flour, plus 250g/9oz/

1⅔ cups for kneading
1.5 litres/2½ pints/6 cups warm water
200ml/7fl oz/scant 1 cup olive oil
1 small bunch of rosemary

Mix the yeast and salt evenly through the flour in a large bowl, then make a well in the middle of the flour. Using a wooden spoon, gradually add the warm water, stirring constantly until you have a slurry-like, vaguely lumpy-looking paste (this is what we call a 'loose dough'). Make sure that there are no clumps of unmixed flour in the dough.

Heavily flour a 60cm/24-inch area of work surface. Add extra flour to your hands (ideally wearing disposable gloves). Pour the wet dough into the centre of the floured area, sprinkle more flour liberally over the top and sides, then gently start bringing the dough together. Keep gently lifting and folding, adding a little flour at a time, until the dough is even, silky and no longer semi-liquid.

Pour half the oil into another mixing bowl. Drop the dough into it, then turn it over a couple of times to ensure it is completely covered with the oil. Cover the dough with a tea towel and leave for 45 minutes, after which you will have created a monster!

Preheat the oven to 200°C/400°F/gas mark 6. Take a couple of heavy non-stick pans or oven trays (any shallow, heavy vessel will do) and pour 2–3mm/⅛ inch of oil into the bottom of each. Divide the dough between them and leave it to rise again for 5 minutes. Now, deeply stipple the dough with your fingers, creating pockets for oil to pool in, and pour the rest of the oil over the top of each tin. Nestle spears of rosemary in a random fashion over the top of the dough and sprinkle generously with sea salt.

Bake for 25–30 minutes, or until the focaccia is a deep golden colour and golden on the underside when tipped out of the tin. For best results, drizzle the loaf with a little more oil as soon as it comes out of the oven. Leave to cool on a wire rack for 1 hour.

IRISH SODA BREAD

Makes 1 loaf   *All year round*

Soda bread is unique. Traditionally a poor-man's bread from Ireland, it has now attained something akin to cult status. Nothing quite compares to the nutty aroma of baking or cooling soda bread.

It has great advantages for the modern cook over normal types of bread, in that it requires no proving or rising. The basic principle, of course, is that it uses baking soda and buttermilk in place of yeast. The most important thing to remember when making it is to do as little kneading as possible; the looser the dough, the better. Traditionally, the cross-shaped cut on top of the soda bread was made to bless the bread and the corners were pricked to allow the fairies to escape.

450g/1lb/3¼ cups strong white (white bread) flour (to
    make brown soda bread, use half wholemeal (wholewheat)
    flour and half white flour), plus extra to dust
1 tsp salt
1 tsp bicarbonate of soda (baking soda)
350–400ml/12–14fl oz/1½–1¾ cups sour milk or
    buttermilk, to mix

Preheat the oven to 230°C/450°F/gas mark 8.

Sift the dry ingredients into a bowl. Make a well in the centre. Pour most of the milk in, then using one hand, mix in the flour from the sides of the bowl, adding more milk if necessary. The dough should be softish, not too wet and sticky.

When it all comes together, turn it out on to a well-floured work surface, then pat the dough into a round about 4cm/1½ inch thick. Put a cross on it and prick the corners. Put on a baking tray (sheet).

Bake for 15 minutes, then turn the oven down to 200°C/400°F/gas mark 6 and bake for a further 30 minutes, or until cooked. If you are in doubt, tap the bottom of the bread – if it is cooked, it will sound hollow. Cool on a wire rack.

APPLE AND PEAR CHUTNEY

Makes 10 x 500ml/18fl oz jars   *Autumn*

The key to chutney-making is to think big. It's going to take a long time to cook, so you might as well make a lot of it. This chutney is a brilliant one to make in the Autumn, when there is a glut of apples and pears.

Chutney keeps for ages and improves with time, so don't be afraid of having lots of jars of it. When you perfect the recipe, you will inevitably be giving it to your friends, for nothing makes a better gift than a jar of homemade chutney.

You must invest in a stainless-steel pan, because aluminium will discolour when it comes into contact with the fruit and sugar. I do not peel my apples and pears for a chutney; I leave the skin on because somehow it is more rustic. How large your pieces of fruit are depends upon the texture you like.

2 cinnamon sticks

2 star anise

4 cloves

2 medium-hot red chillies (chiles)

4 bay leaves

30 cloves of garlic, unpeeled

3kg/6½lb eating (dessert) apples, cored and finely diced

3kg/6½lb pears, cored and finely diced

1 thumb-sized piece of fresh root ginger

6 white onions

1.5 litres/2½ pints/6½ cups malt vinegar

1kg/2¼lb/5 cups soft dark-brown sugar

sea salt and freshly ground black pepper

Place all the spices and the bay leaves in a muslin (cheesecloth) bag and tie it up with string.

Remove the root end from each clove of garlic. Place them in the stainless-steel preserving pan, along with the spice bag, all the fruit, ginger and onions and bring it up to a medium heat. Add the vinegar and sugar. Simmer for 4–5 hours, until most of the liquid has disappeared.

Taste the chutney and check the seasoning. Then, using a jam funnel, pour it into warm Kilner jars that have been washed in hot soapy water and sterilized in an oven preheated to 160°C/300°F/gas mark 3 for 10 minutes. Seal with vinegar-proof tops and store in a cool, dark place.

Leave for 3 months before consuming. Once the jar has been opened, keep it in the fridge and consume within 1 month.

THYME AND PARSLEY BUTTER FOR ROASTS

Makes 250g/9oz *All year round*

The older I get, the less I like a beautiful piece of meat covered in sauce or gravy. A thin slice of beautifully flavoured butter melting over said cut of meat is more than enough, and this concoction is one that I use for venison, pork, lamb and game birds. The technique is simple and the result should be kept in the freezer, where it will be ready for instant use and last perfectly for up to three months.

250g/9oz/1 generous cup butter (softened), roughly chopped
1 tbsp finely chopped thyme
1 tbsp finely chopped flat-leaf parsley
1 tbsp finely chopped chives
zest of 1 unwaxed lemon

Mix everything together in a mixing bowl by hand or using an electric whisk until the ingredients are thoroughly combined.

Lay two sheets of clingfilm (plastic wrap) on a work surface and spoon the butter mixture down the centre. Roll up into a 4cm/1½-inch tube and twizzle until tight. If you wish, cut it into quarters and keep it in freezer bags. If only one or two portions are required, take a couple of slivers off and just melt with a blowtorch (removing the clingfilm first!).

Check the butter is hard, remove the clingfilm and wrap in greaseproof (wax) paper or a non-plasticised polyethylene film.

TARRAGON AND BASIL BUTTER FOR FISH

Makes 250g/9oz   *All year round*

This little recipe is seriously useful, and with adaptations (see left) can be an accompaniment to loads of meat and fish dishes. Just decide what flavourings you like and go for it. The key is to keep it in the freezer until you need it. This butter in all its forms can go on fish, meat, in Kievs or on veg.

250g/9oz/1 generous cup butter (softened), roughly chopped
2 cloves of garlic, grated
1½ tsp finely chopped flat-leaf parsley
1½ tsp finely chopped tarragon
1½ tsp finely chopped basil
1½ tsp sea salt
½ tsp ground black pepper

Mix everything together in a mixing bowl by hand or using an electric whisk until the ingredients are thoroughly combined.

Lay two sheets of clingfilm (plastic wrap) on a work surface and spoon the butter mixture down the centre. Roll up into a 4cm/1½-inch tube and twizzle until tight. If you wish, cut it into quarters and keep it in freezer bags. If only one or two portions are required, take a couple of slivers off and just melt with a blowtorch (removing the clingfilm first!).

Check the butter is hard, remove the clingfilm and wrap in greaseproof (wax) paper or a non-plasticised polyethylene film.

INFALLIBLE VINAIGRETTE

Makes 250ml/9fl oz/scant 1¼ cups   *All year round*

This vinaigrette is the base for my pigeon salad on page 84. When you have practised making it a few times you won't need to use quantities; just do it by eye. This is a very French style of dressing, which means it is thick, keeps well and is so delicious that you can eat it just with bread.

50ml/2fl oz/¼ cup extra-virgin olive oil
150ml/5fl oz/scant ¾ cup vegetable oil
2 heaped tbsp wholegrain mustard
juice and zest of 1 unwaxed lemon
2 tbsp white wine vinegar
1 tbsp runny honey
sea salt and freshly ground black pepper, to taste

Put all the ingredients into a mixing bowl and whisk together vigorously to emulsify. Pour into a couple of sterilized jars or bottles (see page 228), seal and keep in the fridge. Shake before each use. It keeps for a month.

BASIC GREEN SAUCE

Makes 150ml/5fl oz/scant ⅔ cup   *All year round*

Green sauce is one of my favourite things to have on simply cooked meats and fish. It also makes a good dressing for hot potatoes and veg – a real multipurpose condiment.

3 anchovies in oil
1 small bunch of basil
1 small bunch of chervil
1 small bunch of flat-leaf parsley
1 clove of garlic, grated
1 tbsp baby capers
100ml/3½fl oz/scant ½ cup extra-virgin olive oil
zest and juice of 1 unwaxed lemon
sea salt and freshly ground black pepper

It is important to do the knife-work by hand for this little recipe – texture is crucial and the herbs mustn't be destroyed in a food processor. Finely chop the anchovies and herb leaves, then put them into a bowl. Add the garlic, capers, oil and lemon juice and zest, season to taste and stir to combine. Keep in a sealed sterilized jar (see page 228), chilled, and use within 3 days.

INDEX

ACKNOWLEDGEMENTS

Two entirely different worlds came together to make this book possible – those of television and media, and those of the countryside.

From the media, I would like to thank my agent Martine Carter, my commissioning editor at Anova, Becca Spry, and Mike Blair, David Fewster, Diana Howie, Paul Freeman and Kevin Morgan at ITV, who all made this possible. I'd also like to thank Kristin, Pene, Sam and Kostas, who made the photos so marvellous. Also a big thanks to all the film crews and producers I have worked with over the last two years.

From the country, I would like to thank all the farmers and producers we have filmed with, as well as the landowners and gamekeepers who have allowed me to practise my skills on their lands. You know who you are!

I would like to thank my business partners Kate Robinson, Oli Shute, Brett Graham and Edwin Vaux for their patience and forebearance whilst I was writing this tome, and particularly my mentor and friend, the great Alan Hayward of Vicars Game, who taught me all I know about deer, shooting and butchery.

Finally to my parents Alan and Gilly Robinson, who have always let me follow my own path and who have been endlessly supportive, and to my best friend and canine companion Sassy, without whom I would be lost... thank you.